Ethnic
Minorities

London: H M S O

ISBN 0 11 701650 0

HMSO publications are available from:

HMSO Publications Centre
(Mail and telephone orders only)
PO Box 276, London, SW8 5DT
Telephone orders 071-873 9090
General enquiries 071-873 0011
(queuing system in operation for both numbers)

HMSO Bookshops
49 High Holborn, London, WC1V 6HB   071-873 0011 (counter service only)
258 Broad Street, Birmingham, B1 2HE   021-643 3740
Southey House, 33 Wine Street, Bristol, BS1 2BQ   (0272) 264306
9-21 Princess Street, Manchester, M60 8AS   061-834 7201
80 Chichester Street, Belfast, BT1 4JY   (0232) 238451
71 Lothian Road, Edinburgh, EH3 9AZ   031-228 4181

HMSO's Accredited Agents
(see Yellow Pages)
and through good booksellers

Photo Credits

Numbers refer to the pages in the illustration section (1–4): Format Partners
front cover (top); Metropolitan Police front cover (bottom right), p. 2 (bottom);
Press Association p. 3 (top); BBC Pebble Mill p. 3 (bottom). Department of the
Environment p. 4 (bottom left and bottom right).

Contents

Introduction

The most notable social change in Britain in the period
after the second world war (1939–45) has been the settlement
of substantial immigrant communities, mainly from former
colonies in the Caribbean and the South Asian sub-continent.
Migrant workers were similarly attracted to most other
industrialised Western European countries, and the assimilation
of people with different cultures, many of them speaking
different languages, has not been without difficulties. Britain[1]
is now a multiracial society with an ethnic minority population
of about 2·58 million—some 4·7 per cent of the total population
—of whom about 45 per cent were born in Britain.

Arriving in the 1950s and early 1960s the newcomers
settled in the inner cities where, at the time, employment
opportunities were greatest and housing was cheapest. The
economic base of these areas was already declining, however,
leaving many members of the black and Asian communities
disproportionately concentrated in areas of greatest deprivation
and social stress. The disadvantages that they shared with
poorer sections of the indigenous population have been compounded by racial discrimination. During the early to mid-
1980s some of these areas were the scene of urban disorders,

---

[1] The term 'Britain' is used informally in this book to mean the United
Kingdom of Great Britain and Northern Ireland: 'Great Britain' comprises
England, Scotland and Wales.

highlighting a breakdown in confidence between the police and certain members of the community, both black and white.

Successive governments have been committed to the principles of equality before the law and equality of opportunity. Efforts to alleviate racial disadvantage are being made through the social, economic, educational and environmental programmes of central and local government which have channelled substantial expenditure into the regeneration of the inner cities. Measures are now being taken to involve local people more closely in deciding on priorities and on targeting funds more effectively. At the same time, against a background of legislation that makes discrimination unlawful in employment, education, housing and the provision of goods and services, policies are being pursued to promote equality of opportunity for all citizens.

While progress has undoubtedly been made over the last 25 years, it is acknowledged that for many it has not been fast enough. Although members of the ethnic minorities increasingly participate in all areas of national life, many others continue to lack the opportunity to overcome the disadvantages they experience. Nevertheless, much enterprise is being shown by black and Asian people to improve the well-being of their communities. Policies for tackling the problems of the inner cities are designed to encourage self-help and voluntary action in creating a greater sense of community. Moreover, a growing number of institutions, including local authorities, public bodies, firms, companies and trade unions, are taking stronger action to ensure that opportunities are equally available to all.

This book outlines some of the action being taken by the Government and others to combat disadvantage, including special measures in employment, education, the health and social services, and housing. It refers to what is being done to improve relations between the police and the ethnic communities. There is also a brief description of the press and broadcasting services for the ethnic minorities and of their activities in the arts.

Terminology presents some difficulty in that while many ethnic minority people prefer to use the all-embracing word 'black', in certain contexts it is more helpful to distinguish between black or Afro-Caribbean and Asian groups. The latter course has been taken in this book where a distinction is relevant. Even so, within these broad groups are people from a diversity of religions, languages and cultural backgrounds.

Background to Immigration

Because of its long tradition of accommodating immigrants and refugees and because it is part of a multiracial Commonwealth, Britain contains a diversity of peoples. In London, the capital, students and business people from overseas add to the numbers of nationalities resident there and the city is among the most multiracial in the world. It has been estimated that some 160 languages and dialects are spoken by children in London schools. For many centuries a variety of people have been absorbed into British society, having come to Britain in search of better economic opportunities or to escape political or religious persecution. Huguenots (French Protestants) settled in the seventeenth century as did Jews from the continent of Europe in the nineteenth. The Irish have long formed a substantial part of the population. Refugees from Nazi Germany arrived in the 1930s before the second world war. After the war large numbers of refugees and displaced persons, Poles in particular and subsequently Hungarians, entered Britain.

The presence of some black immigrants was recorded in the sixteenth century. In the seventeenth and eighteenth centuries young black people were brought to Britain as domestic servants. Former slaves from the Caribbean followed, and black seamen have traditionally settled in ports such as Liverpool, Bristol and Cardiff. Substantial immigration from the Caribbean, India, Pakistan and Bangladesh[1] began in the 1950s at a time when the other countries of Western Europe were also receiving large numbers of immigrants from less industrialised parts of the world. In addition, in 1972, Britain admitted some 28,000 Asians expelled from Uganda and, in the late 1970s, some 18,000 refugees from South-East Asia. Chinese immigration developed in the nineteenth century with seamen settling in London and Liverpool. It continued after the second world war and accelerated, especially from Hong Kong, in the 1960s. Significant numbers of Italians, Greek and Turkish Cypriots, Australians, New Zealanders and people from the United States and Canada are now resident in Britain.

Afro-Caribbean people came to Britain from all of the widely scattered islands in the Caribbean which are in the Commonwealth, as well as from the mainland territories of Guyana and Belize. Nearly 60 per cent came from Jamaica. Although they share a colonial history, the people of each country regard themselves as distinctive from the others. Their mother tongue is English, although a variety of dialects are spoken, and they mainly adhere to Christian denominations. In the 1950s and 1960s job opportunities were better in Britain than in their own countries and some of those who came had served in the Royal Air Force during the second world war or had worked as skilled craftsmen in factories on Merseyside.

---

[1] Pakistan formerly consisted of two separate parts—East and West Pakistan. In 1971 East Pakistan became the new state of Bangladesh and joined the Commonwealth in April 1972. In January of that year Pakistan (formerly West Pakistan) had withdrawn from the Commonwealth but rejoined in October 1989.

Others were recruited by London Transport for work on the buses and the Underground railway.

Immigration from India and Pakistan (including Bangladesh) began a little later than that for the Caribbean and reached its peak in the late 1960s, prompted by a desire for better opportunities in employment and education. Among Asians there is a great variety of religions, language and culture, and the family remains a strong institution. Most Indians have come from the Punjab and Gujarat. Their languages include Punjabi, Gujarati, Urdu and Hindi. Many of those of Asian origin from East Africa are also Gujarati, mainly descended from Indians who migrated to East Africa as businessmen or to work in railway construction. Those who came to Britain from Pakistan speak Urdu and Punjabi while those from Bangladesh speak Bengali. Religious groupings cross the national divisions. While Muslims, Hindus and Sikhs are the most numerous, the Asian community also includes Christians.

Until 1962 Commonwealth citizens had always been free to enter Britain as they wished. In that year, however, the Government decided that it was necessary to limit the number of immigrants to a level the country could absorb, both economically and socially, and the first legislation to control Commonwealth immigration was passed. Further restrictions were introduced in 1968, and entry from all countries is now controlled by the Immigration Act 1971 (as amended by the British Nationality Act 1981 and by the Immigration Act 1988) which is administered under immigration rules made in accordance with the Act.

Reflecting these restrictions, the overall level of immigration has been decreasing. Recent settlement totals have been markedly lower than in the mid-1970s. In round terms they fell from over 81,000 in 1976 to 70,000 in 1979, to 55,000 in 1985 and 46,000 in 1987, while slightly increasing to 49,000 in 1988 and 1989.

The majority of those accepted for settlement are spouses or dependants of people who are British citizens, or who are settled or settling in Britain. In recent years, around a half of those accepted were wives and children, and about a further one-sixth were husbands. Of the total accepted for settlement in 1989, 22,900 (47 per cent) were citizens of the New Commonwealth;[2] 7,900 (16 per cent) were citizens of Old Commonwealth countries; and 18,300 (37 per cent) were from other countries. The geographical areas from which the largest numbers came were the South Asian sub-continent (12,400), the rest of Asia (9,400), Australasia (6,800) and Africa (6,400).

Numbers and Demographic Characteristics

Pending the publication of the results of the 1991 Census of Population (see p. 26), the most up-to-date statistics on ethnic minority populations come from the *Labour Force Survey*.[3] This is a sample survey and the results from the 1986, 1987 and 1988 surveys have been averaged to avoid sampling error. During this period, the total ethnic minority population of Great Britain was about 2·58 million (some 4·7 per cent of the

[2] That is, all countries of the Commonwealth (including Pakistan) except Australia, Canada and New Zealand—the 'Old Commonwealth'.
[3] The Labour Force Survey is an annual survey of private households. It includes questions about ethnic origin and country of birth. Results in this section are based on interviews conducted between 1986 and 1988 with some 180,000 households.

total population of 54·5 million) of whom about 45 per cent were born in Great Britain. Table 1 indicates the population by ethnic grouping, including the percentage of those born in Britain for each group. Ethnic group does not necessarily equate to birthplace. The survey indicated that 18 per cent of the Indian population resident in Great Britain were born in East Africa (mainly Kenya and Uganda) and that two-thirds of the resident overseas-born Chinese were born in Hong Kong, Malaysia and Singapore.

The survey also gives information about the age structure of the population and shows the predominance of children and young adults in the ethnic minority population. The proportion of people aged under 25 in the white population was 33 per cent, while it was 48 per cent in the Afro-Caribbean and Indian populations, 60 per cent among Pakistanis and 63 per cent in the Bangladeshi population. The population of mixed ethnic origin had the youngest age structure of all: over half their number were aged under 15 and three-quarters under 25. Out of the total ethnic minority population, only 4 per cent had reached pensionable age (65 for men and 60 for women), while about 19 per cent of the white population were in this group.

Statistics compiled from birth registrations show that, because of the relatively youthful age structure of the ethnic minority groups, births to mothers born in the New Commonwealth and Pakistan accounted in 1988 for 7 per cent of all live births in England and Wales. This proportion rose steadily through the 1970s (from 5·8 per cent in 1971 to 8·5 per cent in 1980) but has fallen gradually since. These figures exclude births to women from the ethnic minority populations who were themselves born in Britain. Fertility rates (births per 1,000

Table 1: Population by Ethnic Group, Great Britain, 1986–88 Average

Ethnic group	Thousands All persons	Percentage born in Britain
White	**51,470**	**96**
All ethnic minority groups	**2,577**	**45**
Afro-Caribbean	495	53
Indian	787	37
Pakistani	428	46
Bangladeshi	108	32
Chinese	125	26
African	112	38
Arab	73	14
Mixed	287	77
Other	163	36
Not stated*	472	68
All groups	**54,519**	**93**

Source: *Labour Force Survey*.
* There is evidence that most survey respondents in the 'not stated' category are white.

women aged 15 to 44) fell for all women between 1971 and 1985, most markedly for those born in the Caribbean and India—by 46 per cent and 36 per cent respectively compared with 29 per cent for women born in Britain. The fertility rate for Caribbean-born women is now only slightly higher than that of the population at large.

Geographical Distribution

The *Labour Force Survey* indicates that the highest concentration of ethnic minorities is in Greater London and the six metropolitan counties of England, areas where employment opportunities were greatest at the time of the initial arrival of immigrants. Some 71 per cent of the ethnic minority population live in Greater London and the metropolitan counties compared with 31 per cent of the white population, and over 43 per cent live in Greater London itself compared with only 11 per cent of the white population.

Table 2 shows the estimated distribution of population resident in Greater London and the metropolitan counties by ethnic group. After Greater London, the next largest concentration of Indians and Afro-Caribbeans is in the West Midlands (including Birmingham) while more Pakistanis have settled in West Yorkshire than elsewhere. The table indicates that the proportion of ethnic minority groups living in the metropolitan counties ranges from 55 per cent of the Chinese population to 83 per cent of the Afro-Caribbean.

Apart from the concentration of the ethnic minority groups in London and in towns within the metropolitan counties (Birmingham, Wolverhampton and Coventry in the West Midlands, Manchester and Bolton in Greater Manchester, and Bradford in West Yorkshire), large communities are found in Leicester, Slough, Luton and Blackburn.

Scotland has proportionately fewer people from the ethnic minorities than elsewhere in Britain. They number about 43,000, according to *Labour Force Survey* statistics. The main ethnic groups comprise Pakistanis (17,000), Indians (5,000), Arabs (5,000) and Chinese (4,000). There are smaller numbers

Table 2: Population Resident in Greater London and Metropolitan Counties by Ethnic Group, Great Britain, 1986–88 Average

Thousands

Ethnic group	Metropolitan county of residence					All met. counties	Great Britain	Per cent living in met. counties
	Greater London	Greater Manchester	West Midlands	West Yorkshire	Other met. counties			
White	**5,462**	**2,397**	**2,256**	**1,856**	**3,736**	**15,707**	**51,470**	**31**
All ethnic minority groups	**1,100**	**134**	**326**	**162**	**77**	**1,800**	**2,577**	**71**
Afro-Caribbean	288	20	77	18	7	410	495	83
Indian	333	36	130	38	8	546	787	69
Pakistani	72	47	70	80	13	282	428	66
Bangladeshi	51	4	17	5	7	84	108	78
Chinese	51	5	1	2	9	69	125	55
African	77	2	3	2	6	91	112	81
Arab	31	3	4	3	6	48	73	66
Mixed	104	13	18	11	15	160	287	56
Others	92	3	5	4	6	110	163	67
Not stated	**78**	**29**	**18**	**13**	**32**	**170**	**472**	**36**
All groups	**6,640**	**2,560**	**2,600**	**2,031**	**3,845**	**17,677**	**54,519**	**32**

Source: *Labour Force Survey.*

of Africans (2,000), Afro-Caribbeans (1,000) and Bangladeshis (1,000). People of mixed race number about 6,000.

Northern Ireland has very few ethnic minority groups. According to the 1981 census (the latest available figures), Indians living in Northern Ireland numbered just over 1,200 and Chinese people about 740.

Ethnic Minorities in Society

Members of the ethnic minorities as a whole, in particular black and Asian, experience a number of social disadvantages to a greater extent than other groups. Their children are more likely to need special help in education. Unemployment is higher among the ethnic minorities than among the population at large, this disparity being particularly acute within the younger age groups. These difficulties have been compounded by unfamiliarity with British society and, especially among Asian groups, by differences in language and culture. In addition to social disadvantages, there are also the effects of racial discrimination in certain areas of life.

A major concern of successive governments has been to promote equality of opportunity for all groups and to remove discrimination. The main economic, social, educational and environmental programmes are designed to bring about improvements in many of the inner city areas. Special measures have been taken to help with difficulties arising, for example, out of language and cultural differences and to give help to the unemployed. Legislation against discrimination was first introduced in 1965. Its scope was widened by the Race Relations Act 1968, which made discrimination in employment, housing and education, and in the provision of goods, facilities and services, unlawful. The law was further strengthened by the Race Relations Act 1976 which introduced the concept of 'indirect discrimination'. This may be found in practices which unintentionally or otherwise disadvantage particular racial groups, and those responsible may be unaware of its existence.

The effectiveness of the legislation has been the subject of much research and examination. Discrimination has diminished in some important respects but not in others, necessitating continued efforts to eradicate it. The chairman of the Commission for Racial Equality (see p. 29), in a review of the organisation's activities during 1988, said that, while there should be no complacency about the scale of the problem, he was encouraged by the commitment of so many authorities, organisations and individuals to eradicating racism and discrimination.

Such a recognition within British society of the harmful effects of racial discrimination should not be obscured by the publicity sometimes given to the activities directed against ethnic minority communities by a small number of extremist groups and individuals.

Achievements in Public Life

Though racial disadvantage persists, it is by no means universal. Increasingly members of the ethnic minorities are achieving distinction in public, professional and commercial life, in the arts and in sport.

Public Office

The House of Commons now has five ethnic minority members. Keith Vaz and Ashok Kumar, who are of Asian origin, represent the constituencies of Leicester East and Langbaurgh. The three black members are Diane Abbott, Paul Boateng and Bernie Grant, who represent the London constituencies of Hackney

North and Stoke Newington, Brent South and Tottenham respectively. Asian members of the House of Lords include Lord Chitnis, Lord Sinha, Lord Desai, Lady Flather and Lady Dunn, while Lord Pitt, a black peer, was born in Grenada. Lady Flather, who is of Indian origin, took her seat as Britain's first Asian woman peer in June 1990. She was formerly a magistrate and barrister and has been active in public voluntary service, sitting on a number of committees of inquiry and advisory bodies. In 1976 she was the first woman from the ethnic minorities to become a local government councillor. Lady Dunn, who is of Hong Kong Chinese descent, took her seat in October 1990. She holds various company and public appointments and is a member of the Hong Kong Executive Council. Lord Desai took his seat in June 1991.

The number of black and Asian councillors in local government has been increasing, and several London boroughs and towns outside the capital have had black or Asian mayors. The London borough of Lambeth has a black Chief Executive, Mr Herman Ouseley, and Mr Gurbux Singh is Chief Executive of the borough of Haringey.

The Professions
In the professions a growing number of black and Asian people are achieving distinction. In law, for example, two Circuit Judges and a number of Recorders of the Crown Court are of ethnic minority origin, as are an estimated 6 per cent of practising barristers. In 1988 Mr John Roberts, who was born in Sierra Leone, and Mr Leonard Woodley from Trinidad became the first black barristers to be appointed Queen's Counsel. Patricia Scotland became the first black woman

Queen's Counsel in March 1991. There is increasing black and Asian representation in the magistrates' service, where the positive commitment to equal opportunity has been the subject of a Home Office initiative launched in March 1989. Mrs Pauline Crabbe, a prominent social worker and broadcaster, is a magistrate of long standing, as was the Rt Rev Wilfred Wood before his appointment as a suffragan bishop in the Church of England in 1985.

In medicine members of the ethnic minorities are well represented, both as hospital and family doctors and in the nursing profession. Dr Farrukh Hashmi, a consultant psychiatrist, has served on many boards and committees, and Professor Magdi Yacoub, who was born in Egypt, is a prominent consultant in heart surgery.

In teaching a growing number of schools have black head teachers. Mrs Yvonne Conolly, who comes from Jamaica, is Senior Inspector for Primary Education in the London borough of Islington. Miss Jocelyn Barrow, who was born in Trinidad, is a distinguished educationist, a former member of the Board of Governors of the British Broadcasting Corporation (BBC) and now deputy chairman of the Broadcasting Standards Council. In higher education many academic posts are held by members of the ethnic minorities. Dr Indraprasad Patel was Director of the London School of Economics and Political Science from 1984 until 1990; Professor Bhikhu Parekh is professor of political theory in the University of Hull; Professor Stuart Hall is professor of sociology in the Open University; and Professor Abdus Salam of the Imperial College of Science and Technology was a joint winner of the Nobel Prize for Physics in 1979.

The Media

In the media Trinidad-born Trevor McDonald, appointed in 1973 as the first black newsreader, is currently with Independent Television News (ITN). Moira Stuart, London-born of Bermudan and Barbadian parents, has been a newsreader with the BBC since 1981. Zeinab Badawi, of Sudanese origin, has been a presenter on ITN's Channel 4 news programme since 1989. Asian and black broadcasters and journalists are well represented in local radio and in the provincial and minority press.

The Arts and Entertainment

Established black actors and actresses include Hugh Quarshie of the Royal Shakespeare Company, Oscar James and Norman Beaton, while the talents of others such as Vicky Licorish and Josette Simon have been more recently acknowledged. Asian actors include Zia Mohyeddin, Saeed Jaffrey and David Yip. Madhur Jaffrey is an actress and presenter of cookery programmes on television. Alby James has become Britain's leading black theatre director, and Lenny Henry remains one of the most popular comedians. Indian-born artist Anish Kapoor was selected to represent Britain at the 1990 Venice Biennale. Playwrights such as Farrukh Dhondy, Mustapha Matura and Michael Abbensetts have achieved distinction. The talents of Winsome Pinnock, a young Jamaican playwright, have also been recognised. Prominent among the many writers whose work has received acclaim in Britain are Trinidad-born V. S. Naipaul, Buchi Emecheta from Nigeria and Salman Rushdie, of Indian extraction, who won the Booker Prize for Literature in 1981.

Black performers who have recently made an impact in pop music include Billy Ocean, Sade, Mica Paris, Yazz, Ruby Turner, Roland Gift, and groups such as Aswad and Soul II Soul. Tanita Tikaram is considered a gifted singer/songwriter, and the jazz saxophonist Courtney Pine is highly acclaimed. In classical music Sandra Browne and Patricia Rosario have achieved success as opera singers and the composer Shirley Thompson has gained recognition.

Commerce and Public Service
The ethnic minority communities have shown enterprise in a variety of commercial undertakings, especially shops, restaurants and small businesses. Particularly successful businessmen and entrepreneurs from the South Asian sub-continent and from East Africa include Mr Swraj Paul, who is chairman of a large group of companies with interests in engineering, hotels, property and shipping; Mr Jasminder Singh, a hotelier; Mr Roy Sandhu, a property developer; Mr Shami Ahmad, owner of a Manchester-based clothing concern; and Mr Yaqub Ali, Scotland's most successful Asian businessman. Mr Narindar Saroop holds various company and public appointments and is on the council of the Institute of Directors. Mr Pranlal Sheth is a company director and a trustee of various organisations, and Mr Praful Patel, who has been active in immigrant welfare work, is a company director and investment adviser. Mr Suresh Choksi is a major figure in the London diamond trade.

Other prominent figures from among the ethnic minorities include Mr Prabhu Guptara, a management consultant who has been elected to the council of the British Institute of Management and is a member of the Commonwealth Trust; Mr Viren Sahai, who has achieved distinction in town planning, architecture and painting; and Mr Chaman Lal Chaman, with a varied career in broadcasting and welfare work. Valerie Amos was appointed as chief executive of the Equal Opportunities Commission in 1989; and Usha Prashar is director of the National Council for Voluntary Organisations.

In view of their present under-representation on public bodies such as consumer councils and advisory committees, members of the ethnic minorities are being actively encouraged by the Government to seek public appointments as an important element in the process of integration.

Black and Asian people have been increasingly active within the trade union movement. The most prominent national official from the ethnic minorities is Mr Bill Morris who, in June 1991, was elected general secretary of Britain's biggest trade union, the Transport and General Workers' Union.

Sport

Black sportsmen and women have achieved many distinctions. They are well represented in professional football, and in first-class rugby league, rugby union and cricket. The membership of British athletics teams is now on average about one-third black. John Barnes, Des Walker and Paul Parker are regular players in the England football team. In rugby league Des Drummond, Ellery Hanley and Henderson Gill have represented Great Britain, while Chris Oti and Jeremy Guscott have played rugby union for England and Glenn Webbe for Wales.

Black county cricketers who play for the English Test team include Chris Lewis, David Lawrence and Philip de Freitas.

The outstanding athlete of the last decade has been Daley Thompson, who achieved the world record in the decathlon and won eight consecutive titles in Olympic, World, Commonwealth and European contests. Tessa Sanderson is an Olympic and Commonwealth gold medallist in the javelin. Other black international athletes include Linford Christie, John Regis, Colin Jackson, Kriss Akabusi, Tony Jarrett, Dalton Grant and Judy Simpson.

Chris Eubank is the World Boxing Organisation's world middle-weight champion, while in table tennis Desmond Douglas is a regular international player for England. Corey Roberts became Britain's first black jockey in 1989.

Generally, while the achievements of all these people are to be welcomed and represent real progress in British society, there is still a long way to go before equality of opportunity is achieved in all areas of society.

Alleviating Racial Disadvantage

Strenuous efforts have been made by successive governments and by local authorities, increasingly in partnership with voluntary groups and private bodies, to tackle the problems of racial disadvantage. While the Home Secretary is the minister with general responsibility for race relations matters, each government department places great emphasis on the promotion of equality of opportunity and the elimination of racial disadvantage. The principal means of combating such disadvantage is through the main programmes of expenditure for which government departments are responsible. These comprise:

—the Urban Programme and associated schemes administered by the Department of the Environment;

—the employment and training programmes of the Department of Employment;

—the schemes of regional and industrial assistance run by the Department of Trade and Industry; and

—the educational and health services for which the Department of Education and Science and the Department of Health are responsible.

In Scotland the Urban Programme, regional and industrial assistance and educational services are the responsibility of the Scottish Office.

There are two main sources of funds which channel extra resources specifically to ethnic minorities—the so-called 'Section 11' grants and the Urban Programme. In addition, the Home Office makes grants to strengthen national or key local organisations whose work reduces racial disadvantage.

Home Office Grants

Under Section 11 of the Local Government Act 1966 local government authorities may receive grant to help them employ extra staff to meet the special needs of communities of New Commonwealth origin. Home Office grant supports 75 per cent of the salary costs of such staff and local authorities make up the remainder. In 1988–89, £89 million was paid in grant to local authorities, supporting some 12,000 posts, with provision for £110 million in 1990–91. About 80 per cent of grant supports education posts, mainly for the teaching of English as a second language. The remainder provides funding in such areas as social services, business development, and interpretation and translation.

Following an efficiency scrutiny into Section 11 administration, the Government in October 1990 announced new funding arrangements to take effect from April 1992. These aim to promote practical projects working to identified needs, to be monitored against recognisable performance targets. Local authorities are strongly encouraged to work with voluntary organisations. Separate funding for some innovative projects will be co-ordinated with the new Training and Enterprise Councils (see p. 43) supported by Task Forces and City Action Teams (see p. 24).

The Urban Programme

The Urban Programme gives specific grant through local authorities to some 10,000 projects a year to help deal with special needs in inner cities. Since 1979 the emphasis of the Urban Programme has shifted. Increasingly it is used to support capital projects which will strengthen and revive the local economy, foster enterprise and improve the environment of run-down areas in order to rebuild confidence and encourage private investment. The Urban Programme is targeted on priority groups and areas through local strategies drawn up by the local authorities in consultation with the private sector and local voluntary and ethnic minority groups.

Ethnic minorities have been identified as a priority group within the inner city. Since 1980–81 over £250 million has been directed to projects of specific benefit to them. In 1989–90 the total of Inner Area Programme expenditure was £259·6 million of which £30·5 million (about 12 per cent) was spent on projects of specific ethnic minority benefit. Nearly 1,000 projects were being funded, of which about 80 per cent were run by voluntary organisations. Of these:

—45 per cent of expenditure was allocated to projects for health, welfare, culture and recreation, and for education;

—44 per cent to economic projects;

—7 per cent to housing schemes; and

—4 per cent to environmental schemes.

Examples of such projects include the Black Business Development Association, providing advice, training and small grants to ethnic minority businesses; and a scheme in the London borough of Tower Hamlets establishing a computer suite to provide local unemployed people from the Bangladeshi community with information technology skills. Another project primarily of benefit to ethnic minorities involves the conversion of a warehouse building in the London borough of Hackney into workshop units for start-up businesses. There are also many broad-based projects which help ethnic minorities without specifically catering for them.

In Scotland the Urban Programme can also be used to support ethnic minority projects in areas of multiple deprivation, although funds are not set aside specifically for this purpose.

City Action Teams

Another initiative directed at certain inner city areas where the problems are most severe was the establishment in 1985 of five 'City Action Teams'—one each for London, Birmingham, Liverpool, Manchester/Salford and Newcastle upon Tyne/Gateshead (now covering Tyne and Wear). Three more teams have since been set up, covering Cleveland, Leeds/Bradford and Nottingham/Leicester/Derby. They aim to co-ordinate the government programmes in these areas in co-operation with the local authorities and private and voluntary sectors in order to ensure that the maximum advantage is gained from the considerable government expenditure. The City Action Teams strive to help local residents in gaining access to training and employment, encourage the growth of new and existing businesses and try to improve the condition of housing and the local environment. Each City Action Team has a small budget, a total of £7·8 million in 1990–91, to assist in this. The City Action Teams are co-ordinated by the Department of the Environment.

Task Forces

In addition to City Action Teams, 16 locally based inner city Task Forces operate in the most deprived urban areas. They aim to help local communities by improving the targeting of government help in their areas and, in particular, by developing innovative approaches to stimulate employment and enterprise. They also support schemes which improve the environment or help to reduce crime where these are linked directly to the provision of training or jobs. A key feature, as with the City

Action Teams, is encouraging the involvement of the private sector, local authorities and the voluntary sector in this process.

The first eight Task Forces were set up in 1986 and a further eight in 1987. Task Forces are not intended to be permanent. A number have already been closed and others opened as part of a rolling programme. From late 1991, there will be Task Forces operating in North Kensington/ Hammersmith, North Peckham, Deptford and Hackney in London, Hull, Coventry, East Birmingham, South Tyneside, Middlesbrough, Moss Side and Hulme in Manchester, Nottingham, Bristol, Bradford, Granby/Toxteth in Liverpool, Derby and the Wirral.

Many of the projects supported by Task Forces are designed to meet the special needs of ethnic minorities. Examples include a project in Deptford to help members of the Vietnamese community gain access to Department of Employment programmes and acquire job search/interview techniques and a project in East Birmingham aiming to develop bilingual skills for Asian women and to provide experience of computing, language and classroom work for a classroom assistant's training course. Other examples include the provision of access training into management for black people in Granby/Toxteth, and of high-quality training to unemployed ethnic minorities to enable them to gain employment in the health service in Moss Side, Manchester.

The Task Forces are co-ordinated by the Department of Trade and Industry and had a budget of £23·2 million in 1990–91.

1991 Census of Population

The 1980s have seen the increasing acceptance of ethnic monitoring, and a question on ethnic origin was included for the first time in the Census of Population taken in Britain in April 1991. A census test which included a question on ethnic group was conducted in areas of London, Birmingham, Scarborough, Edinburgh, Berwickshire and East Lothian in 1989 and indicated that the question commanded a high degree of acceptance from all the main ethnic groups. Such statistical information, it is believed, will help central and local government and health authorities to allocate resources and plan programmes, taking account of the needs of each group. It should also help employers and those providing services to identify and tackle areas of racial disadvantage. The ethnic categories in the 1991 Census question were the same as the classification recommended by the Commission for Racial Equality, namely:

1. White
2. Black—Caribbean
3. Black—African
4. Black—Other
   (to be specified)
5. Indian
6. Pakistani
7. Bangladeshi
8. Chinese
9. Other (to be specified)

Detailed statistics, compiled from the Census, will be published in stages from late 1991.

Race Relations Legislation

Policies to remove racial disadvantage and promote equality of opportunity are pursued against a background of legislation against racial discrimination. The Race Relations Act 1976, which applies to England, Scotland and Wales, makes racial discrimination unlawful in a wide range of circumstances.

Definition of Discrimination

Under the Race Relations Act 1976 two kinds of conduct are regarded as racially discriminatory:

—direct discrimination means treating a person less favourably on 'racial grounds', that is, for reasons of colour, race, nationality or ethnic or national origins; and

—indirect discrimination constitutes treatment which may be described as 'equal in a formal sense as between different racial groups, but unjustifiably discriminating in its effect on one particular racial group'.

It is unlawful to discriminate in:

—employment, in areas of recruitment, terms and conditions of work, promotion and dismissal;

—education;

—the provision of goods, facilities and services; and

—the provision of housing and accommodation, recreational amenities and finance.

It is also unlawful to pursue 'discriminatory practices' in which indirect discrimination may occur although there is no identifiable victim. Such practices may include discriminatory advertisements, instructions or pressure to discriminate, or aiding discrimination. Segregation on racial grounds is regarded as racial discrimination. The Act makes it unlawful for clubs and associations of 25 members or more to discriminate in the selection of new members. It also places a duty on local authorities to carry out their functions in such a way that discrimination is eliminated and equality of opportunity and good race relations promoted.

There are a number of general exceptions to the Act, for example, in order to comply with charitable instruments, for employment in a private household or in order to meet the needs of a particular racial group in education, training or welfare.

The Act does not permit 'reverse discrimination'. This means discrimination in favour of a person of a particular racial group, for example, in recruitment or promotion, on the grounds that members of that group have in the past suffered from adverse discrimination. It does, however, permit certain forms of positive action in particular circumstances. This may take the form of training and encouragement of persons of a particular racial group to take advantage of opportunities for doing work in which they are under-represented.

Enforcement

People who consider that they have been discriminated against have the right to institute proceedings in a designated county court (a sheriff court in Scotland). Cases involving discrimination in employment, partnerships, trade unions, qualifying bodies and employment agencies are dealt with by an industrial tribunal. If proceedings are taken, the remedies available from the courts are the award of damages, including damages for injured feelings; an order declaring the rights of the parties; or an injunction (or order in Scotland), ordering a particular person or body to perform, or not to commit, or to stop committing, specified acts.

An industrial tribunal will send a copy of a complaint concerning discrimination in employment to the independent Advisory, Conciliation and Arbitration Service which may try to help the parties reach a settlement without the need for a tribunal hearing. If the case does reach a hearing, the tribunal can declare the rights of the parties, recommend that the respondent take a particular course of action, and award compensation, including damages for injured feelings.

It is unlawful to victimise people who assert their rights under the Act or to help others to do so.

Commission for Racial Equality

The Act set up the independent Commission for Racial Equality with responsibilities for working towards the elimination of discrimination, for promoting equality of opportunity and good relations between people of different racial groups and for keeping under review the Race Relations Act.

The Commission has the power to assist individuals to bring complaints of discrimination before the courts or industrial tribunals. Such help may include giving advice, seeking a settlement or arranging for legal advice, assistance or representation. It has sole responsibility for bringing proceedings in connection with discriminatory practices, advertisements and pressure to discriminate and it has powers to deal with persistent discrimination.

The Commission also has power to conduct 'formal investigations' for any purpose connected with its duties. If in the course of an investigation it is satisfied that the Act has been contravened, it can issue a non-discrimination notice on the people concerned, which is enforceable in the courts by way of an injunction or order requiring that such practices cease.

Codes of Practice

In employment, the Commission has issued a code of practice for eliminating racial discrimination and promoting equality of opportunity. This gives practical guidance to employers, trade unions and others on the provisions of the Act. The code came into force in 1984.

The Housing Act 1988 gave the Commission statutory authority to issue a code of practice in the area of rented housing, in both the private and public sectors. The code offers a guide to the law, and outlines ways of avoiding racial discrimination, promoting equal opportunity, countering racial harassment, training housing workers and taking positive action. The Local Government and Housing Act 1989 extended the Commission's statutory code-making powers to the non-rented area of housing, including estate agents, lending institutions and valuers.

A non-statutory code of practice for the elimination of racial discrimination in education was published in December 1989 and has been endorsed by the Secretary of State for Education and Science. The code outlines the application of the Race Relations Act to education and is being widely distributed to education authorities, schools, colleges and governing bodies. It applies to England and Wales; a Scottish code is in preparation.

Grants

The Commission has power to make grants to voluntary and self-help organisations, both national and local, concerned with the promotion of equality of opportunity and good race relations. During 1990 the Commission distributed short-term project aid among 24 such organisations, contributing mainly to the salary and administrative costs involved in running advisory and liaison projects. Eight organisations were in receipt of long-term project aid during 1989–90.

Research

The Commission also undertakes research itself and finances research undertaken by others, concentrating on projects that directly assist its promotional, investigative and advisory work. In 1989, for example, it commissioned a project on race and the administration of justice, which is being carried out by the Institute of Criminology at Oxford University. A register of race research is being compiled for publication.

The Commission is financed by a grant from the Home Office, expenditure in 1990–91 totalling over £13·5 million. An annual report is prepared for the Home Secretary and laid before Parliament.

Review of Legislation

After a long period of consultation with representatives of particular interest groups, the Commission for Racial Equality published in 1985 proposals for changes to the legislation (*Review of the Race Relations Act 1976: Proposals for Change*). In making its recommendations the Commission stated that, although it believed that the structure and general thrust of the legislation was right, its intention was to make the present Act work better. The proposals were substantial and complex, and raised issues affecting the responsibilities of many government departments. The Government has considered these proposals but has stated that no major changes to the race relations legislation are planned. It is ready, however, to change the law where necessary.

Race Equality Councils

At local level, the Commission for Racial Equality supports a network of over 80 race equality councils (formerly community relations councils) employing over 600 staff. These are voluntary bodies which aim to promote equality of opportunity, good race relations and the elimination of racial discrimination. The councils, the first of which were set up in the early 1960s, are usually composed of representatives of statutory and voluntary bodies, including the churches, trade unions and ethnic minority organisations committed to racial equality.

In 1990–91 nearly £4 million was allocated to councils by the Commission in grant aid for the employment of race equality officers and assistants, with a further £290,000 in discretionary and supplementary grant aid. Most councils receive additional financial assistance from their local authority.

In 1988 the Policy Studies Institute published a research report on the role and objectives of community relations councils (as they were called at that time). The Commission undertook widespread consultation on the report's conclusions, as a result of which councils were invited to opt into a 'new partnership for racial equality' with the Commission by the end of July 1990. The vast majority of councils have opted in and are being reconstituted as race equality councils. As a result of these changes, there will be closer collaboration between the Commission and the councils in joint planning, investigations, law enforcement and promotional work.

Incitement to Racial Hatred

The Race Relations Act 1976 strengthened the criminal law on incitement to racial hatred by inserting a new clause into the Public Order Act 1936. This has been reinforced and extended by the Public Order Act 1986: the previous offence of incitement by the use of threatening, abusive or insulting words or behaviour or the publication or distribution of such material *likely* to stir up racial hatred has been redefined to cover such matter or behaviour *intended* to stir up racial hatred. The offence is punishable by fine and/or imprisonment. In England and Wales a prosecution may be brought only by, or with the consent of, the Attorney-General.

The 1986 Act also created a new offence of possessing racially inflammatory material with a view to its publication or distribution. The police have been given new powers of search and seizure in relation to such material and the courts are now able to order its forfeiture. The law also covers broadcasting, cable and other media involving visual image and sound recording.

Racial Harassment

The terms 'racial harassment' and 'racial attacks' cover a wide range of offences from verbal abusiveness and graffiti to physical assault and arson. The Government is committed to combating racial harassment, and has published the Report of an Inter-Departmental Racial Attacks Group, which provides guidelines for individual agencies such as the police, social services, housing departments and local education authorities, and also recommends that a multi-agency approach to the problem ought to be instituted locally.

Advice and Research

An Advisory Council on Race Relations advises the Home Secretary on the development and implementation of race relations policies. It also provides a forum for ministers to discuss matters of concern with members of the ethnic minority communities and representatives of interested organisations. Within the Home Office there are two Community Relations Consultants who provide specialist advice on race and community matters, including advice on the implications of race relations for the police, probation, fire and prison services. The

Department of Employment has a Race Relations Employment Advisory Group which advises ministers on matters relating to the employment of the ethnic minorities.

The need for factual information about matters concerning race relations on which to base policy decisions is reflected in the volume of research undertaken by government departments, official bodies including local authorities and race equality councils, academic institutions and other independent organisations. The Home Office has a Research and Planning Unit which undertakes studies to assist the department in its administrative functions and funds policy-related research by universities and other agencies. There is also a research branch in the Department of Employment.

Besides undertaking research themselves, government departments commission other bodies to carry out studies on their behalf. In particular, the Scottish Office has commissioned a major survey of Scotland's ethnic minority population. Research is also supported by the Economic and Social Research Council, mainly through specific grants. It funds the Centre for Research in Ethnic Relations based at Warwick University. The Commission for Racial Equality has published the results of many studies, often in its quarterly periodical *New Community*. Major inquiries have also been carried out by the Home Affairs Committee of the House of Commons. These include a study of the Bangladeshi community in Britain, published in 1987, and a report on racial attacks and harassment, published in 1989.

Independent institutions which have published research studies on questions related to the position of ethnic minorities include the Policy Studies Institute, the National Foundation for Educational Research, the Runnymede Trust and the Minority Rights Group.

The Council of Churches for Britain and Ireland (formerly the British Council of Churches) has a long-established Community and Race Relations Unit, and the Society of Friends addresses racial issues through its Community Relations Committee. The Catholic Association for Racial Justice has a publications programme in progress. A major Church of England report on the problems of the inner cities and other areas of social deprivation entitled *Faith in the City* was published in 1985. A second report, *Living Faith in the City*, was published in January 1990.

Employment

Policies to enable the ethnic minorities to compete for work on equal terms have been formulated by the Department of Employment. These efforts to alleviate disadvantage and discrimination have been supported by the trade unions, many large employers and the Commission for Racial Equality. The role of the Department of Employment is to increase employers' awareness and understanding of the race relations legislation and to encourage them to give equal opportunity to the ethnic minority groups, both in respect of access to work and to progress within employment.

Employment Patterns and Status

According to the averaged results of the 1986, 1987 and 1988 *Labour Force Surveys* (see p. 7), about 4·8 per cent of the population of working age[1] in Great Britain (1·6 million people) are from ethnic minority groups. The results also indicate that each group has a distinctive pattern of involvement in the labour market. Among young people in the 16 to 24 age range, economic activity rates are lower in the ethnic minority groups (57 per cent overall) than in the white population (79 per cent). These differences are partly explained by the higher proportion of young people from the ethnic minorities staying in full-time

---

[1] 16 to 64 years of age for males and 16 to 59 for females.

education and partly by the different proportions of young women, particularly Pakistanis and Bangladeshis, whose family and domestic activities mean that they are not available for work. The proportion of economically active adult men is generally high—88 per cent for whites and 79 per cent for ethnic minority groups. Among women in the 25 to 59 age range about 75 per cent of Afro-Caribbeans are in the labour force,* compared with 67 per cent of white women and 55 per cent of Indians. Women of Pakistani and Bangladeshi origin have much lower economic activity rates. This appears to be related to religious and cultural differences.

Of the economically active members of the ethnic minority community, 59 per cent live in the South East region, including nearly two-thirds of Afro-Caribbeans, more than half of Indians, and more than a third of Pakistanis and Bangladeshis. This compares with 31 per cent of the corresponding white population.

The employment status of people in work varies with ethnic origin. Overall, 82 per cent of men of working age in employment are employees, 15 per cent are self-employed and 2 per cent are on government schemes. For Asian men the proportion of self-employed is higher than average (27 per cent for Indians and 23 per cent for Pakistanis and Bangladeshis) while Afro-Caribbeans are the least likely to be self-employed (9 per cent). Among women, 7 per cent of those in employment are self-employed, including 12 per cent of those of Indian origin. Among women employees, full-time work is more commonly undertaken by the ethnic minority groups while part-time work is more prevalent among the white population.

Types of Work

There is some degree of concentration of ethnic minority groups in particular industries and occupations, although they are represented in most sectors. For example, 29 per cent of men from ethnic minority groups are employed in distribution, hotels, catering and repair work, compared with 16 per cent of white workers. Ethnic minority men are also well represented in the health services and in the transport and communications industry. Smaller proportions are employed in construction, public administration, agriculture and fishing. Among women, the ethnic minorities are more likely to be working in the health services and in parts of the manufacturing sector, particularly the clothing and footwear industry.

For men in employment, the proportions of ethnic minority workers in non-manual and manual occupations (46 and 54 per cent respectively) are very similar to the proportions for white workers. However, there are considerable variations among the different ethnic groups: 54 per cent of Indian men are in non-manual occupations, compared with 28 per cent of Afro-Caribbeans and 36 per cent of Pakistanis and Bangladeshis. A converse pattern applies for manual occupations: the proportions in craft and similar occupations were 29 per cent for the Afro-Caribbean group, 19 per cent for Indians and 17 per cent for Pakistanis and Bangladeshis. Among women in employment, a slightly higher proportion of the white population than of other ethnic groups are in non-manual rather than manual occupations, while Indian women were more likely than others to be in skilled manual work.

Qualifications

People from ethnic minority groups are, overall, less likely than white people to have formal qualifications of some kind, but a slightly greater percentage of them hold higher qualifications (above GCE A-level or equivalent). Among the ethnic groups, people of Pakistani and Bangladeshi origin are the least likely to possess qualifications, while men of Afro-Caribbean origin also tend to be less qualified. Younger people in these groups are better qualified than their older counterparts.

Unemployment

Unemployment rates for ethnic minority groups are appreciably higher than those for the white population—17 per cent for the ethnic minorities and 10 per cent for white people. There are wide variations from these overall figures among the different ethnic groups and according to age and sex. The highest unemployment rates are among the Pakistani and Bangladeshi communities and among 16- to 24-year-olds in each of the main ethnic minority groups.

Action to Remove Disadvantage

Research has shown that discrimination, though not always conscious or intentional, affects both recruitment and promotion prospects of members of ethnic minority groups. Against the background of the Race Relations Act, policies to promote equality of opportunity are pursued by government departments, by the Commission for Racial Equality and by an increasing number of public and private sector employers. The Commission's code of practice in employment, issued in 1984 (see p. 30), provides a framework against which employers may review their personnel policies, practices and procedures to ensure they are free from racial bias. Statements of support for equal opportunity policies have been made by the Confederation of British Industry and the Trades Union Congress. Many public bodies, businesses and local authorities have declared themselves 'equal opportunity employers'.

Ethnic Monitoring

'Ethnic monitoring' is acknowledged as an important means of ensuring that equal opportunity policies are being put into practice. Such monitoring can help to identify whether and where discrimination is taking place so that remedial action can be taken.

Between 1985 and 1988 the Civil Service carried out nationwide surveys to monitor the ethnic origin of all civil servants. These showed that while black, Asian and other ethnic minority staff were joining the Civil Service in proportion to their numbers in the working population, they were not yet reaching the highest levels. As a result, in May 1990 the Government announced a programme to strengthen equal opportunities in civil service departments and agencies for people of ethnic minority origin. The programme, which is building on existing policies, covers recruitment and selection procedures, training, development and promotion.

Other employers in the public and private sectors have also introduced ethnic monitoring procedures. For example, such monitoring began in 1991 throughout the probation service.

Contract Compliance

'Contract compliance' is also regarded as a mechanism for promoting equal opportunity policies. All government contracts contain a clause which states that a contractor shall not discriminate within the meaning and scope of the Race Relations Act and shall take all reasonable steps to ensure the observance of these provisions. How effectively this clause is being observed has been a subject of discussion. The Local Government Act 1988 gave a statutory basis to the use of contract compliance schemes by local authorities and to the encouragement of private contractors to adopt equal opportunity policies.

Positive Action

The Race Relations Act contains provisions for 'positive action' in certain circumstances. Under the Act employers and other bodies may give encouragement and training to people from particular racial groups to help them gain access to work in which they have been under-represented during the previous year. Employers may also offer training to employees from a particular racial group to fit them for work in which that group has been under-represented, or may encourage people from that racial group to take advantage of opportunities for doing that work.

'Positive action' gives considerable scope for opening up job opportunities and improving career development for ethnic minority employees. Employers benefit by reaching a wider labour market and realising under-used potential.

Race Relations Employment Advisory Service

Since 1968 the Department of Employment has operated a free and confidential Race Relations Employment Advisory Service. The role of the Service is to promote equal opportunity in employment within the terms of the Race Relations Act. Advisers are based in areas of high ethnic minority settlement. They provide employers with advice and practical help in developing and implementing effective equal opportunity strategies, including awareness training for senior managers and personnel staff, and the introduction of ethnic monitoring. The Service is also giving greater publicity to the use of the 'positive action' provisions of the Race Relations Act.

Training

The Training Education and Enterprise Division of the Department of Employment is responsible for the Government's training programmes, to which members of the ethnic minorities have equal access. In England and Wales a new network of employer-led Training and Enterprise Councils has the task of developing the quality, effectiveness and relevance to the labour market of the Government's training and enterprise programmes. In Scotland, local enterprise companies are providing a similar service.

Employment Training is the main adult training programme. Intended primarily for people aged 18 to 29 and unemployed for over six months, the scheme aims to provide a broad range of training; to increase employers' involvement in adult training; and to encourage self-development. It includes provision for people who need training in English as a second language. The Youth Training programme offers vocational training to young people leading to national vocational qualifications. Both Employment Training and Youth Training have equal opportunities codes of practice.

A commitment to equal opportunities, underpinned by a contractual requirement, is one of the criteria for achievement of approved training organisation status.

Co-operation with voluntary agencies to provide courses for young adults is encouraged. The Fullemploy Group was set up in the mid-1970s to improve the employment prospects of ethnic minorities in England and Wales. It runs training courses for young adults, supports community and economic development among black communities, and offers employers a range of consultancy and training services in setting up equal opportunities ventures.

The Windsor Fellowship supports ethnic minority undergraduates wishing to follow management careers. The Fellowship recruits young people with self-motivation, leadership qualities and with GCE A-level qualifications, and then matches them with potential employers who sponsor them while they are studying for a degree.

Ethnic Minority Business Initiative

The Ethnic Minority Business Initiative, partly financed by Section 11 funds and by Home Office grants to alleviate racial disadvantage (see p 21), was established in 1985 to finance local enterprise agencies aiming to ease the entry of ethnic minority enterprises into the mainstream of British business. Five local enterprise agencies were set up in Deptford, Finsbury Park and Wandsworth in London, Handsworth in Birmingham, and in

Bristol. The costs of 'outreach workers' in a further six agencies are now funded by the initiative.

The initiative funded two recent conferences aimed at breaking down barriers to ethnic minorities in business. An ethnic minority business development team, staffed by secondees from a bank and a number of government departments, was also set up. This works in selected multiracial areas to help increase the contacts and flow of business between ethnic minority entrepreneurs and the wider community. The team's work is due to end in 1991–92.

Other Initiatives

A community affairs section of the Prince's Youth Business Trust, which encourages small firms and self-employment, has been formed to give financial assistance and advice to aspiring young ethnic minority business people. The Trust offers grants and loans to people aged between 18 and 25 to start or develop small businesses. The Department of Employment has supported the Trust, matching private sector donations to the sum of £40 million and providing secondees to give advice.

A government-backed mentor scheme in north London, the first of its kind in Britain, partners young ethnic minority students with successful black professionals and business people who act as role models.

Trade Unions

The Trades Union Congress (TUC) and many individual unions favour policies to promote equal opportunity and have taken steps to put such policies into practice. In recent years there has been much more activity within the TUC on race relations issues. It has a race relations advisory committee, has published a *Charter for Black Workers* and has produced a considerable amount of multilingual trade union literature.

In 1989 a slightly lower proportion of male ethnic minority employees than their white counterparts (39 per cent as opposed to 44 per cent) were members of trade unions, though the reverse was true for female employees. Employees of Afro-Caribbean origin, both male and female, are more likely than other ethnic groups, including white people, to be trade union members. This is partly due to the greater propensity of this group to work in industrial sectors with high rates of union representation. Among employees overall, ethnic minorities accounted for nearly 5 per cent of trade union membership in 1989.

Participants in the multi-ethnic Notting Hill Carnival, Europe's biggest street carnival, which celebrated its 25th anniversary in 1990.

Members of 'Kokuma', one of Britain's prominent Afro-Caribbean performing arts companies.

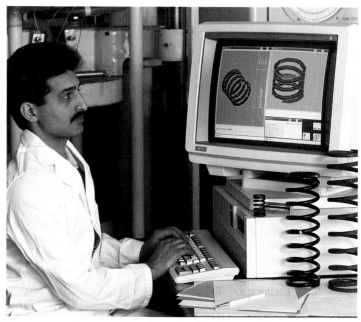

A systems consultant engaged in advanced engineering research at Leeds Polytechnic.

Metropolitan Police officers on the beat.

Bill Morris, general secretary-elect of the Transport and General Workers' Union, Britain's largest trade union.

Danny Choranji presenting BBC Radio 5's 'Eastern Beat' for Britain's Asian youth.

British Muslim schoolchildren at the Commonwealth Institute celebrating Eid-ul-Fitr, the day of rejoicing that marks the completion of Ramadan.

Dr B's, a thriving Caribbean restaurant in the Chapeltown area of Leeds.

The Nari Samity Women's Centre in Tower Hamlets, established with Urban Programme assistance, serves the Bangladeshi community.

Education

Most of the children from the ethnic minorities now starting school were born in Britain and they share the aspirations and interests of children in the population at large. Nevertheless, many of them still experience difficulties arising from cultural differences, including those of language, religion and customs. In addition, the concentration of some ethnic minority communities in the inner city areas where social and economic deprivation are most severe has meant that many of them share with others the educational disadvantage associated with such areas.

Government Policies

The Government believes that everyone should have the same opportunities to fulfil their educational potential, and aims to ensure that the education service meets the particular needs of the ethnic minorities. Education is compulsory for children between the ages of 5 and 16 in Great Britain and 4 and 16 in Northern Ireland. Most children attend schools within the state system which are free for all pupils, including those who stay on beyond the minimum leaving age. Just under half of three- and four-year-olds receive education in nursery schools or classes or infants classes in primary schools. Many children also attend pre-school playgroups. For those who have left school, a wide range of courses is available in colleges of further and higher education, polytechnics and universities.

In 1985 the Committee of Inquiry into the Education of Children from Ethnic Minority Groups, under the chairmanship of the late Lord Swann, published a major report entitled *Education for All*. This heralded government action to reduce the underachievement among some ethnic minority pupils and to improve the responsiveness of the education service to ethnic diversity. Initiatives included action on initial and in-service teacher training; measures to increase recruitment of ethnic minority teachers; funding for pilot projects directed at meeting educational needs in a multi-ethnic society (see p. 53), including some designed specifically to promote good race relations; and action on the curriculum and examinations. Good practice in the teaching of English to those who do not speak it as their mother tongue has also been encouraged.

Ethnic Monitoring

The Government has acknowledged the need for statistics on the ethnic origins, language and religions of schoolchildren as a means of ensuring that education meets the needs of all pupils, thereby helping to secure equality of opportunity. In September 1990, local education authority-maintained and grant-maintained schools began to collect ethnically based information provided voluntarily by parents covering 5- and 11-year-old pupils. Returns are submitted to the Government annually.

Inspections

Routine inspection of schools and colleges is carried out by Her Majesty's Inspectors, who assess trends and standards and report to the Government. In England some inspectors have specific responsibilities concerning educational responses to ethnic diversity; there is a staff inspector with national responsibility who leads a team of regionally based specialist inspectors for whom this is a component of their work. The inspectors direct the Department's annual programme of short courses for teachers which regularly includes courses on education in an ethnically mixed society. They also take part in conferences arranged by local education authorities and other educational bodies.

In Scotland one inspector has a national responsibility for monitoring developments in multi-ethnic education in schools and colleges, while another has a similar remit in relation to informal further education. Inspectors have helped to plan national courses on multi-ethnic education. They also contribute to courses and conferences arranged by divisional and regional education authorities.

Schools

The Government believes that the education service needs to equip ethnic minority groups with the knowledge, skills and understanding to participate fully and on equal terms in all aspects of British life, while maintaining their own cultural identity. The Government has also made it clear that racial discrimination has no place in the education service. A code of practice for the elimination of racial discrimination in education, published by the Commission for Racial Equality in 1989 (see p. 31), was endorsed by the Secretary of State for Education and Science.

For children whose parents do not speak English in the home, the first priority is to acquire a fluent command of

English. Local education authorities and schools have made extensive provision for English language support to meet this need. Provision is also increasingly being made for the support of mother-tongue teaching in schools, especially in the early primary years, as a means of ensuring access to the curriculum and facilitating the acquisition of English.

National Curriculum

The Education Reform Act 1988 provided for the introduction, in stages from September 1989, of a broad and balanced National Curriculum for children aged 5 to 16 in all state schools in England and Wales and for regular assessments of performance. The National Curriculum consists of the core subjects of English, mathematics and science, and other foundation subjects, offers equality of opportunity and aims to promote the development of all pupils. National criteria for the General Certificate of Secondary Education (GCSE—the main vehicle for testing National Curriculum subjects at age 16) require that syllabuses and examinations should be free of ethnic bias. Remits to the National Curriculum Council and to the Schools Examination and Assessment Council require them to take account of the ethnic and cultural diversity of British society and of the importance of promoting equal opportunities for all pupils regardless of ethnic origin and gender. The Scottish Examination Board applies similar criteria. The school curriculum in Scotland is not statutorily prescribed but guidance to education authorities recommends a curriculum which promotes mutual understanding between individuals of different ethnic and cultural origins.

A modern foreign language is a National Curriculum foundation subject at secondary level. The languages which qualify as the foundation subject include the working languages of the European Community, together with Arabic, Bengali, Gujarati, Hindi, Japanese, Mandarin or Cantonese Chinese, Modern Hebrew, Punjabi, Russian, Turkish and Urdu. All schools must offer a working European Community language and may also offer one of the other listed languages. Where a choice of foundation subject language is offered, parental preferences about what each pupil studies should be taken into account.

Religious Education

Religious education forms part of the basic curriculum throughout Britain. Syllabuses must reflect the fact that the religious traditions in Britain are mainly Christian while taking account of the teaching and practices of the other principal religions. Schools in England and Wales are also required to provide a daily act of worship. This must be of a broadly Christian character, though there is flexibility for this requirement to be lifted if the head teacher considers it inappropriate for some or all pupils.

In Scotland guidance has been issued to education authorities recommending that religious education and observance in schools should be similarly based on Christianity while promoting understanding of and respect for those who adhere to different faiths.

Children may be withdrawn from religious education classes and acts of collective worship if parents wish.

Parental Choice

The Government attaches great importance to meeting parents' wishes about the education of their children. A number of measures have been taken in the last ten years to widen the choice of schools available and to increase parental involvement in school organisation.

The Education Act 1980 gives parents a statutory right to express views about the school they would like their children to attend and local education authorities are under a duty to meet the parents' wishes. The Education Reform Act 1988 requires schools to admit pupils up to the limit of their physical capacity from September 1990: this policy, known as 'more open enrolment', will further increase parental choice of schools. Both Acts provide a stronger base for Muslim families, in particular, seeking admission to a single-sex school and make it easier for families where there are no such schools to apply to schools in neighbouring authorities' areas.

Questions have arisen in certain areas where there is a concentration of Muslim children over the dress of Muslim girls, sex education and the availability of 'Halal' meat (meat from an animal slaughtered according to Islamic law). These matters have been the subject of local discussion and in some cases special arrangements have been made. In Bradford, for example, where there is a large concentration of Muslim schoolchildren, guidelines have been issued to the schools by the local education authority, 'Halal' meat is available, and single-sex schools have been established.

Liaison between the schools and the home is considered important. Many authorities with significant ethnic minority populations have made particular efforts to forge such links, often by appointing home–school liaison officers and encouraging parental involvement in other ways. It is also considered important that the governing body of a school should reflect the community it serves. In some areas parent governors from among the ethnic minorities have been appointed. Recent legislation gives parents greater involvement in schools by providing for equal representation of elected parent governors and governors appointed by local education authorities. Provision is also made for a statutory category of co-opted governors to strengthen links with the local community.

The legislative background to schools organisation in Scotland rests on similar principles embodying parental choice and diversity of provision.

Grants

Substantial funds have been made available to local education authorities to meet the special needs of ethnic minority pupils and students. Grants are made by the Home Office under Section 11 of the Local Government Act 1966 (see p. 21), of which more than 80 per cent of expenditure in 1989–90 was on education, amounting to nearly £76 million. The Urban Programme also provides funding for educational projects of specific benefit to ethnic minorities (see p. 22). The Education Support Grant programme supported expenditure of about £2·3 million in 1990–91 on projects related to the educational needs of a multi-ethnic society.

City Technology Colleges

City technology colleges, sponsored by industry and commerce, are being set up in urban areas in England and Wales to provide broadly based secondary education with a strong technological and business element. They are state-aided but independent of local authorities. Managed by sponsors from universities and commerce, educational trusts, charities and other voluntary organisations, the colleges are intended to enhance the educational opportunities of children, particularly in the disadvantaged inner cities.

Teachers

Teacher-training institutions have long been encouraged to ensure that students are adequately prepared for teaching in a multi-ethnic society, and initial training courses offer relevant studies including training for teaching English as a second language.

In-service training is provided in a variety of ways, from long courses at universities and colleges to short courses at workshops and school-based activities, and including the courses arranged by Her Majesty's Inspectors. For three years from September 1986 the in-service teacher-training grants scheme included 'teaching and the curriculum in a multi-ethnic society' as a national priority area. From 1988–89 there was a comparable national priority area for staff in further education colleges.

The need to encourage more members of the ethnic minorities to enter the teaching profession was also emphasised by the *Education for All* report, which identified the positive contribution they can make to a school through pastoral care, speaking the mother tongue of pupils and serving as a role model. Access courses—special preparatory courses aimed at students from ethnic minorities to enable them to reach the standard necessary for entry into teaching—have proved useful in recruiting a number of students into the profession. The Government has also aimed to attract more ethnic minority members into the profession through advertising and publicity campaigns and exhibitions, and the Teaching as a Career Unit has this as part of its remit. A number of specially designed courses of initial teacher training have also been developed which draw on the linguistic and other skills, experience and qualifications of mature ethnic minority students.

Local education authorities are required to collect statistics on the ethnic origins of the teacher force in order to monitor the effectiveness of these policies and to provide data in support of fair and equal employment opportunities.

Pre-school Education and Play

The provision of nursery education for children aged three and four has been recognised as a valuable means of reducing social disadvantage, particularly when both parents work, and language difficulties may be alleviated in this pre-school period. The number of pupils under five in school in Britain, including those admitted at four to the reception classes of ordinary primary schools, has risen from 340,000 in 1970 to 700,000 in 1988. While it is for the local education authorities to decide what provision for the under-fives they ought and can afford to make, the Urban Programme (see p. 22) is an additional source of support from central funds for nursery education in inner cities.

Post-school Education

Post-school education for young people above school-leaving age is provided in universities, polytechnics and colleges of higher and further education. All abilities are catered for and 'second chance' opportunities are available for people of all ages. A major part of the provision is for vocational education, including courses leading to recognised qualifications, and training for people in employment, some of whom are on technician or craft apprenticeships. Young black people are more likely to continue their education after the minimum school-leaving age than white. This is particularly the case with young Asians and with Afro-Caribbean girls: the proportion of Afro-Caribbean males is also slightly higher than white. In addition, Afro-Caribbean women are more likely than others to undertake part-time study. The special needs of the ethnic minorities in further education are under consideration by the Further Education Unit, an advisory body which is partly funded by the Department of Education and Science.

Further education colleges play an important part in the schemes administered by the Training and Enterprise Councils for the unemployed (see p. 43), including basic courses in literacy and numeracy. They also offer courses designed to provide entry to universities, polytechnics and colleges of higher education other than through the usual GCSE and A-level examinations or Scottish equivalents—for example, access and Business & Technician Education Council (BTEC) courses. They also offer courses in English as a second language, remedial English, extra tuition for people attending other courses, and courses in numeracy.

Adult and Continuing Education

The scope of adult continuing education has broadened in recent years and now covers a wide range of subjects. High priority has been given to work with target groups including adults with literacy, numeracy and basic skills difficulties, including ethnic minority adults. Tuition in English for Speakers of Other Languages (ESOL) is provided for adults with a mother tongue other than English. The number of adults receiving ESOL tuition is increasing, provision by local education authorities and voluntary bodies alone rising from 37,203 in 1985 to 43,916 in 1988. ESOL is mostly provided in small groups, but some individual tuition is available.

Access courses provide an alternative route to higher education for mature students without traditional entry requirements. They are specifically designed to meet the needs of identified groups in the community who may be under-represented in higher education, including ethnic minority adults. The growth of access courses has been very rapid in recent years. It is estimated that about 600 courses were available in 1989.

The Youth Service

Local education authorities and a large number of voluntary organisations provide a range of leisure-time activities for young people designed to promote their personal development and social education. Work with young people from the ethnic minorities is seen as one of the priorities for the Youth Service and it is acknowledged that the service can contribute to countering prejudice and discrimination.

The Urban Programme has provided funds for youth groups in the inner cities, and many self-help groups have been grant-aided by the Commission for Racial Equality. Projects for young unemployed people form an important element in their activities. In 1987, the Commission published a report entitled *Working with Black Youth.*

Social Welfare

The full range of health and personal social services, provided largely free of charge, is available to everyone normally resident in Britain. The various statutory and voluntary bodies concerned aim to deal with any special difficulties experienced by the ethnic minority communities and a number of initiatives directed at specific groups have been undertaken. The social security system provides a range of benefits for people who are elderly, sick, disabled, unemployed, widowed or bringing up children, together with certain income-related benefits for those without adequate means of support.

Health Services

Health Service Delivery
The Government has made clear its commitment to promoting equality of opportunity for ethnic minorities in health service delivery. This involves ensuring that services are accessible and acceptable to people from ethnic minority groups and, where necessary, taking positive action to take account of differences in language, culture and religion. The Department of Health is considering introducing into the minimum data which health authorities have to collect a question on the ethnic origin of patients. The 1991 Census of Population (see p. 26) includes a similar question on ethnic origin. These two sources of information together will, it is believed, provide a useful tool

to health service managers and planners to enable them to provide services appropriate to ethnic minorities.

The Department of Health has commissioned the establishment of a major database on ethnic minority health which will provide information on good practice in the health services and help encourage the development of new services. In 1988 the National Association of Health Authorities published a report entitled *Action not Words*, emphasising the importance of sensitivity and responsiveness in the National Health Service to the various needs of ethnic minorities.

Provision of Care

Health education is a major factor in safeguarding the health of the ethnic minorities. Family doctors, child health clinics and health visitors to the home are all involved in this aspect of health care. The staff of the maternity and child health clinics look after the health of pregnant mothers and children up to school age. After children start school they are the concern of the school health service and the family doctor. A free family planning service is also provided under the National Health Service.

All parents are encouraged to have their children immunised against diphtheria, tetanus and pertussis (whooping cough), measles, mumps and rubella, poliomyelitis and tuberculosis. Advice is also offered on the general care of children, in particular on the importance of a healthy diet.

The rate of perinatal and neonatal mortality among ethnic minorities is higher than among the population as a whole. The Asian Mother and Baby campaign, which ran from 1984 to 1987, was aimed at overcoming barriers of language and culture between patients and health professionals by employing link workers—local women fluent in English and at least one Asian language. The employment of link workers is now extending to other specialities besides maternity and related services, and for other communities with language difficulties.

The incidence of certain diseases is higher among some ethnic minority groups than in the population at large and special measures are being taken to eradicate them. For example, death from coronary heart disease has been shown to be 50 per cent higher than the national average and the Department of Health has produced a video advising ethnic minority communities of the risks of the disease. Health authorities are also encouraged to include information regarding coronary heart disease in their screening and health promotion campaigns for ethnic minorities.

A small but significant number of people in certain ethnic minority groups carry genetic disorders such as sickle cell anaemia and thalassaemia major. Both disorders are currently irreversible and life-threatening. The Department funds the Sickle Cell Society and the Thalassaemia Society to promote awareness of the diseases in ethnic minority communities.

The Department of Health has provided £1 million over a three-year period from 1988–89 for the production of health information materials in various ethnic minority languages. Leaflets, booklets and videos have been commissioned on a wide range of subjects including mental health care, pregnancy, sickle cell disease and thalassaemia. The Department has also funded voluntary organisations to develop information packages in the care of handicapped adults and children, and in maternity care.

Personal Social Services

Local authority social services departments provide or arrange for the provision of personal social services for people with social care needs. The work focuses on the care and protection of children, on families experiencing problems, on mentally and physically disabled people, and on the elderly.

There are vulnerable members of society among the ethnic minority groups just as there are in the rest of the population, but problems experienced by ethnic minorities are sometimes compounded by differences of language, social attitudes and religion. It is recognised that those who deal with ethnic minorities must be aware of these differences, and account is taken of them in the training of social workers. At the same time the recruitment of social workers from the ethnic minorities is encouraged. Although ethnic minority members are well represented in certain sections of the personal social services—for example, working in the home help service and in residential homes for children and adults, particularly the elderly—they have been under-represented in field social work. However, their numbers are now beginning to rise. An increasing number of authorities have created specialist posts for race advisers or development officers.

Families with children aged under five are likely to represent a larger proportion of the ethnic minority population than is the case among the white population. A greater proportion of Afro-Caribbean mothers with children aged under five are in paid employment than other groups and so this group has greater need for full-time day care. It is now generally recognised that from the age of about three children benefit from participating in some form of group activity with their peers and other adults from outside the immediate family circle. It is considered important that children from the ethnic minorities attend a pre-school group because the experience will help to improve understanding of cultural and linguistic differences which might otherwise be obstacles when five-year-olds start school.

Local authorities have a duty to register day nurseries, playgroups and child-minders; under new legislation which came into force in October 1991 they have to impose conditions ensuring that day care services for young children meet accept-able standards.

Local authorities can provide information about the range of services in their area, and some arrange for leaflets, posters and booklets to be available in different languages. Some voluntary organisations target services on children from ethnic minorities. The new legislation mentioned above will also give local authorities a duty to review and publish a report on the day care services in their area. The Department of Health will be issuing new guidance to local authorities which will include advice on services for ethnic minorities.

Where placements are needed or likely to be needed for children from ethnic minority groups or children of a particular religious persuasion, local authorities have been reminded by the Government that it may be necessary to make sustained efforts to recruit a sufficient number and range of foster parents and prospective adopters from those groups and of that religion. This is considered essential if all children who need substitute families are to have the opportunity of placement with families which share their ethnic origin and religion. Local authorities, and other agencies responsible for providing child care services, should take account of the special cultural, racial and linguistic needs of children from ethnic minorities, not only when providing care but also when preparing children for leaving care.

A number of hostels have been established by voluntary organisations for black and Asian young people who have left home or are homeless. Most are financially supported by central or local government. The growing number of elderly people among the ethnic minorities, particularly from the Asian communities, is also receiving attention. A number of social, recreational and sheltered housing projects run by voluntary agencies and local authorities have been established, as well as special schemes such as home helps and domiciliary meal services. A training scheme for voluntary workers with these elderly people has been introduced under the Government's 'Helping the Community to Care' programme.

Voluntary societies have traditionally played an important part in the provision of personal social services, and ethnic minority groups have themselves started a large number of organisations—well over 1,000 are listed by the Commission for Racial Equality. The National Federation of Self-Help Organisations acts as a co-ordinating body for such groups.

Social Security

A number of initiatives have been undertaken by the Department of Social Security to give ethnic minorities information about social security benefits. They include publication of a leaflet entitled 'Which Benefit?' in six Asian languages and Turkish, and the establishment of a free telephone advice and information service in Urdu and Punjabi.

There are training courses for local social security office staff to equip them to serve a multiracial community. Signs and posters have been designed to help ethnic minority callers in local offices and public areas, and an interpreter/liaison service has been set up in Bradford.

Housing

Evidence suggests that the housing conditions of both Afro-Caribbeans and Asians have improved significantly since their initial settlement in Britain although, overall, substantial inequalities between white and black remain.

Types of Tenure

Figures for England, Scotland and Wales indicate quite considerable differences in the type of housing occupied by, in particular, Asians and Afro-Caribbeans and between each group and the white population. While more Asians own or are buying their house or flat—some 73 per cent compared with nearly 63 per cent of white households—Afro-Caribbeans more often live in public sector rented housing—some 41 per cent compared with about 26 per cent of white households. Nevertheless, 49 per cent of Afro-Caribbeans are owner-occupiers. Among Asians as a whole, the proportion of council tenants is low—some 12 per cent.

In the earlier years of settlement, Afro-Caribbeans were more often to be found in rented furnished accommodation or as owner-occupiers of poor quality housing. There has been a noticeable movement from the private rented sector into council housing for Afro-Caribbeans and, for all owner-occupiers, movement into better property. The biggest improvement has been in the much lower proportions sharing houses and occupying housing lacking exclusive basic amenities. For those not living in their own houses or flats or in local authority dwellings, relatively more Afro-Caribbeans and relatively fewer Asians compared with white households are in housing association dwellings (see p. 69).

In Scotland, the Asian community, although small, is found in significant concentrations, mainly in owner-occupied flats in the principal cities. Despite the fact that public sector housing has until recently been the most common form of tenure in Scotland, very few Asian families live in council houses. There is some evidence that ethnic minority households disproportionately occupy overcrowded housing.

House Purchase

Finance for house purchase, in the form of a mortgage (for which the properties are regarded as securities), is most usually obtained from a building society for all groups, though a slightly higher proportion of white purchasers obtain loans from this source. Asian buyers are more likely than other groups to borrow from a bank, and Afro-Caribbeans more likely to borrow from a local authority. A number of building societies have been closely involved in initiatives in inner city areas aimed at improving the housing conditions of all residents, including members of the ethnic minorities.

Private Rented Sector

Over the last 30 years there has been a steady decline in the number of rented dwellings available from private landlords, due to increased owner-occupation, the greater availability of public rented housing and the operation of rent restriction. In order to increase the availability of privately rented accommodation the Government has provided, through the Housing Act 1988 and the Housing (Scotland) Act 1988, for deregulation of new private sector lettings and the introduction of assured tenancies. The previous system of registered fair rents is continuing for existing lettings. The Acts also strengthen the law concerning harassment of tenants by landlords and the illegal eviction of tenants, which are criminal offences.

Local Authority Rented Sector

Most of the public housing in Britain is provided by local authorities. State-assisted housing is also provided by many housing associations (see p. 69). A charter for public sector tenants in England and Wales gives them statutory rights which include security of tenure. Public sector tenants in Scotland have similar rights. Most tenants of local authority housing have the right to buy their accommodation, often at substantial discounts. The 1988 Housing Acts make provision for public sector tenants to choose a new landlord where they are not satisfied with the services provided by their local authority.

Housing policies for the public rented sector pursued by central and local government are intended to ensure a fair allocation of housing between the ethnic groups. However, studies have shown that in many areas there is a tendency for non-white people to be allocated poorer quality accommodation and that cases of direct discrimination do still exist. To counter these problems, improved guidance is now available to local authorities (see 'Housing Advice', p. 72). Local authorities may also apply for grants under Section 11 of the Local Government Act 1966 to meet particular needs. Revised arrangements for these grants were announced in October 1990 (see p. 21). In addition, the Department of the Environment plans to undertake research into the housing circumstances and aspirations of ethnic minorities, reviewing local authorities' practices and procedures.

Housing Associations

Housing associations are non-profit-making organisations which provide accommodation for rent or sale through new building or the rehabilitation of older property. With government encouragement, housing associations have grown in importance in recent years, especially in inner city areas. They cater both for those with special needs and for those outside the owner-occupier or local authority rented sectors.

Housing schemes carried out by associations registered with the Housing Corporation (in England), Scottish Homes or Tai Cymru in Wales qualify for government grant. These three statutory bodies promote, supervise and fund housing associations to provide low-cost homes to those in housing need. Under the 1988 Acts these bodies acquired the duty already placed on local authorities to seek to eliminate racial discrimination and promote equality of opportunity, and a new framework for financing housing associations was established. The grant system was changed to facilitate the maximum use of private sector finance and thereby increase the number of homes that associations can provide for a given level of government grant. The Government has ensured that all associations retain access to sufficient public finance support to ensure the success of their approved development programme.

Some associations, such as the Ujima Housing Association in London and Asian Sheltered Residential Accommodation in Leicester, have undertaken schemes specifically for ethnic minorities. The Federation of Black Housing Organisations provides advice to black groups on setting up specialist housing co-operatives and associations. It has also fostered the development of Positive Action Training in Housing schemes which help housing organisations achieve racial equality and provide trained professional housing personnel from the ethnic minorities.

The Housing Corporation has a programme for encouraging housing associations which specialise in provision for certain ethnic minority groups. By late 1990 it had registered 63 such associations. In January 1990 the Corporation issued a circular outlining its own racial equality strategy and giving advice to housing associations in England on their adoption of similar strategies.

The National Federation of Housing Associations monitors all new lettings made by housing associations through its national CORE (Continuous Recording) system, which includes data on the ethnic origin of households.

Housing Stock Improvement

The emphasis of housing policy in recent years has increasingly been on the better use of existing stock. In the public sector this has meant more priority for better management, and repair and renovation.

The Government's Estate Action programme, set up in 1985, provides local authorities with resources to revitalise their worst housing estates. The programme aims to promote the decentralisation of local authority management to estate level, encouraging greater tenant participation. It also promotes diversification of tenure, the involvement of the private sector, and the linking of housing improvements to the provision of enterprise, training and employment opportunities for residents. Several of the most run-down estates which benefit from the programme have substantial ethnic minority populations. In addition, the Priority Estates Project has developed a model of effective estate-based management and worked with local authorities in applying it to selected estates in England and Wales.

Where social problems and housing disrepair are so serious that greater, more concentrated action is required, the Housing Act 1988 provides for the establishment of Housing Action Trusts. With the consent of tenants, the trusts take over responsibility for local authority housing in designated areas. They renovate and improve it, and then pass it to other approved owners and managers, including housing associations and tenants' co-operatives, or back to the local authority if both the authority and the tenants are willing.

Under the Local Government and Housing Act 1989, local authorities in England and Wales can declare 'housing renewal areas' within which they have powers to acquire land and carry out improvement work. Central government contributes towards expenditure incurred by local authorities in these areas.

A system of house renovation grants has been established in England and Wales under the same Act, primarily to help private owners with the costs of essential repair and improvement work. In Scotland, Scottish Homes has the power to provide improvement and repair grants to complement the role of local authorities in private house renewal.

Housing Advice

Housing advisory centres have been established throughout the country since 1970 by local authorities and voluntary organis-ations. The Department of the Environment has produced a range of booklets giving a guide to major provisions of the housing law affecting private and public tenants. Translations of some of the booklets are available in Bengali, Gujarati, Hindi, Punjabi and Urdu. The Department has also published a guide, based on research commissioned from Brunel University, to help local authority housing departments tackle the problem of racial violence and harassment, which can often occur on local housing estates. The guide gives advice on prevention, victim support and dealing with perpetrators. It also emphasises the need for liaison with the police and other relevant agencies. In 1989 the Department issued advice to all local housing authorities on the Report of the Inter-Departmental Racial Attacks Group (see p. 34).

Under provisions in the Housing Act 1988 and the Local Government and Housing Act 1989, powers were granted to the Commission for Racial Equality to issue codes of practice on race relations in the housing field. The codes will offer guidance on race relations law as it affects housing and will give examples of good practice in the implementation and promotion of equal opportunities. The code of practice for rented housing was issued in May 1991. A draft code covering non-rented housing is currently the subject of public consultation. The Commission has also produced a number of advisory guides on specific aspects of race and housing.

Relations between the Police and the Ethnic Minorities

Since successful policing depends to a great extent on the approval and co-operation of the public at large, there has been widespread concern that relations between the police and some members of the ethnic minorities are not good. The subject of police relations with ethnic minority communities received particular attention after the civil disorders in London in 1981 and again in Birmingham and London in 1985. The report of the inquiry into the 1981 disorders, conducted by Lord Scarman at the request of the Government, said that the disorders could not be fully understood unless they were seen in the context of a complexity of political, social and economic factors, but emphasised the dilemma for the police of how to deal with a rising level of crime while retaining the confidence of all sections of the community. Commenting upon the 1985 disorders, the Commissioner of Police for the Metropolis (London) at that time referred to the social context in which the disturbances occurred as economic deprivation, high levels of unemployment, high rates of crime, and a sense of injustice and discrimination.

To gain the confidence and co-operation of the ethnic minority communities, a number of initiatives have been introduced by the police service. These include measures to increase recruitment of police officers from the ethnic minorities, improved training for police recruits, the formation of community relations departments and policies for tackling racial harassment.

Police Recruitment and Equal Opportunities

There is widespread agreement that the composition of police forces should reflect the society that they serve. The reluctance of members of the ethnic minorities to join the police force has been a cause of concern for many years. At present about 1 per cent of police officers in England and Wales and 1·5 per cent of Metropolitan Police officers are from the ethnic minorities. On the other hand, a much higher proportion—9·8 per cent—of London's Special Constabulary (volunteer police officers who perform police duties as auxiliaries to the regular force) are black or Asian. There are no ethnic minority officers in the ranks of chief superintendent or above, and ethnic recruitment to police civilian jobs has been low.

The Government has accepted the need for a reappraisal of the police recruit selection procedures, and the Police Advisory Board has considered substantial changes in the present entry requirements. All police forces in England and Wales have now abolished minimum height requirements and have recently been provided with the results of research into means of improving recruitment of officers from the ethnic minority communities.

The Government also recognises that effective equal opportunities policies within the police service are essential in order to increase ethnic minority representation. The Home Office issued a circular to police forces to this effect in 1989. While recognising that many forces have already adopted equal opportunities policies, the circular seeks to ensure that all aspects of recruitment, deployment, training and promotion are scrutinised and procedures revised if necessary.

Police Training

The question of police training in race relations has received particular attention since the early 1980s when the recommendations of a Police Training Council working party were commended to the Chief Officers of Police. A new specialist unit, run by an independent training company, was launched in 1989 to provide training organisations, such as the Bramshill Police Staff College, and police forces with practical help and support in community and race relations training. The tasks of the unit include the instruction of police trainers in community and race relations and the establishment of a central bank of training material for use by the police. The unit also develops training strategies and promotes contributions to police training from outside, lay, contributors.

Community Consultation

The Police and Criminal Evidence Act 1984 requires arrangements to be made in each police area for obtaining the views of local people about policing matters and for securing their co-operation in preventing crime. Almost all areas now have police/community consultative groups which enable discussion to take place on issues of local concern. Efforts are made to develop relations with young people through community liaison work in schools and youth clubs. Lay visiting of police stations has been operating successfully in a number of areas, and is an important element in securing greater public awareness of how people who have been arrested are treated by the police.

Racially discriminatory behaviour by police officers is an offence under the Police Discipline Code. Allegations against the police may be pursued through the independent Police

Complaints Authority, established in 1985, or through the civil courts.

Tackling Racial Harassment

The Government is committed to the elimination of racial harassment and believes that it is vital for the police, working with other agencies, to provide an effective and co-ordinated response to racial incidents. In the light of official reports in 1989 by the Inter-Departmental Racial Attacks Group (see p. 34) and the Home Affairs Committee of the House of Commons, the Government is supporting a number of recommendations from the police and other agencies such as local housing authorities and victim support schemes on the effective response to racial attacks. In particular, it has been emphasised that there should be a clear and well-publicised commitment by police forces to tackle racial incidents as a priority, reassuring potential victims and deterring potential harassers. Particular initiatives have been taken by the Leicestershire, Metropolitan, West Midlands and West Yorkshire police services. The Metropolitan Police are also closely involved in a multi-agency project to combat racial attacks in Newham, east London. They are increasingly deploying specialist racial incident squads and mounting *ad hoc* targeted operations. The monitoring of the police response to racial incidents is being stepped up by HM Inspectorate of Constabulary.

Research

In 1989 the Commission for Racial Equality commissioned a two-year research project on race and the administration of justice. The project is being undertaken by the Centre for Criminological Research at Oxford University, with the approval and co-operation of government and other relevant agencies. Also in 1989, following consultation with the Commission for Racial Equality, five police forces agreed to begin ethnic monitoring of police decisions on young offenders and to eliminate any discriminatory practices found as a result. The forces involved are the Metropolitan, West Midlands, West Yorkshire, and Avon and Somerset, which have set up pilot schemes, and Northamptonshire police, which has established a permanent scheme.

Broadcasting and the Press

Broadcasting

The radio and television organisations—the British Broadcasting Corporation (BBC) and the commercial companies broadcasting under the Independent Television Commission and the Radio Authority—aim to reflect the diversity of cultures and languages in British society and provide programmes of interest to all sections of the community.

Television

BBC network programmes for the Asian and Afro-Caribbean minorities are made at the production centre at Pebble Mill, Birmingham. The Asian Programmes Unit has produced a variety of magazine and documentary programmes on television, most recently *East*, a topical weekly broadcast covering Asian affairs in Britain and abroad. It also produces performances of Asian music and dance, and screens drama serials from the South Asian sub-continent. These include the *Mahabharata*, an Indian epic in Hindi, whose 91 episodes are being televised between 1990 and 1992. In 1991 the African-Caribbean Programmes Unit presented *Black on Europe*, a series featuring the black African and Caribbean experience across Europe, and a major six-part documentary series entitled *Black Britain*. It also presented the second series of a black perspective talk-show called *Hear Say* and a four-part documentary series of stories from Soweto in South Africa. In addition, the Religious and Multicultural Programmes Unit produces programmes for network television and radio of interest to ethnic minorities.

More generally, BBC guidelines for programme makers stress the need to avoid unnecessary reference to race or racial origin, to ensure objectivity and accuracy in the coverage of racial questions and to be aware of stereotyped images.

The concerns and interests of the ethnic minorities have also been the subject of programmes made by the commercial television companies. Channel 4 in particular has demonstrated a commitment to multicultural programming in the popular arts, in fiction and in journalism. Many programmes have been made by black producers or companies, such as the magazine series on international current affairs *Bandung File*.

The Broadcasting Act 1990 has a specific requirement for including religious broadcasting on the proposed Channel 3 television network (which will replace the present Independent Television network). Such broadcasting will be required to recognise the range of religious beliefs in Britain. The regulatory bodies will also be able to license religious cable and satellite television channels, subject to safeguards about content, and religious groups will also be able to compete for licences to broadcast on radio.

Radio

Local radio aims to meet the interests of the local population and is playing an increasing part in ethnic minority broadcasting.

There are at present 37 BBC local radio stations, a large proportion of which broadcast regular programmes for ethnic minorities with a mix of local news, views, information and entertainment. For instance, in the South and East region, the magazine programmes *Asian Voice* and *Shararat* are broadcast by Radio Bedfordshire, GLR (Greater London Radio) and Radio Kent. Radio Oxford transmits *Black Voice* for Afro-Caribbean listeners and *Sounds Eastern* for the local Asian community. GLR also caters for ethnic minorities with its daily 'Community AM' broadcasts. In the Midlands region, two-thirds of the local BBC stations provide regular programmes for black and Asian listeners in their schedules. Radio Leicester broadcasts 37 hours of ethnic programmes a week. Some broadcasting is in Asian languages or caters for particular age groups. Radio WM (West Midlands) broadcasts five hours of Asian programmes a day, features BBC World Service bulletins in Urdu and has developed a weekly 90-minute programme in association with Radio 5. It also carries news in Bengali.

Many of the approximately 60 Independent Local Radio stations and 23 incremental community stations also cater for ethnic minority interests. Some, such as Spectrum Radio and Sunrise Radio in London, operate specifically for that purpose. More general broadcasting coverage of the traditions and activities of ethnic groups aims to increase the under-standing of different cultures by the wider audience.

Under the Broadcasting Act 1990 the Radio Authority is able to offer licences for many more independent local stations catering for a range of listeners' tastes and interests, including services for ethnic minorities. The location of the services will depend on demand and the availability of suitable frequencies.

Educational Programmes

Educational programmes from both the BBC and the commercial companies also take account of the ethnic minorities. Many have been designed to help members of ethnic communities cope with day-to-day life in Britain, especially those for whom English is their second language. The BBC has broadcast introductory courses on the Arabic language, and in 1989 transmitted two series—one on television, the other on network radio—to give native English speakers an introduction to Urdu and Hindi. These were designed to appeal to teachers, social workers and health service staff.

Employment and Training

In the areas of employment and training the BBC has adopted an equal opportunities policy, and is taking positive action to increase the number of ethnic minority candidates and their selection. Such initiatives include work experience schemes and a range of training opportunities in journalism and broadcasting production techniques. Radio Leicester regularly funds ethnic training attachments. BBC publicity material and recruitment literature have been revised to reflect a broader ethnic profile. Recruitment procedures have similarly been reviewed.

The Commission for Racial Equality has encouraged the establishment of media access courses for ethnic minority members, and decided in 1989 to fund a training programme for community radio journalists. The Polytechnic of Central London runs a radio journalism course, partly funded by the Government, for ethnic minority students, most of whom have subsequently gained appropriate employment. The Polytechnic has also launched a course in magazine journalism for ethnic minority members, similarly aided by government funding.

The Press

There is a long tradition of immigrant communities starting their own newspapers. Some 100 newspapers and magazines are produced in Britain by members of the ethnic minorities, both in Asian languages and in English. They are mainly produced weekly, fortnightly or monthly. Two Chinese newspapers, *Sing Tao* and *Wen Wei Po*, the Urdu *Daily Jang* (see below) and the Arabic *Al-Arab* are dailies.

English language titles for Asian readers include the weekly *Asian Times* and the recently established *Indiamail*. The English language *Sikh Messenger* and *Sikh Courier* are both produced quarterly. Afro-Caribbean newspapers include *The Weekly Gleaner*, a local edition of the long-established *Jamaican Gleaner*, and *West Indian Digest*. The *Voice* and *Caribbean Times*, both weeklies, are aimed at the black population in general.

Leading ethnic language newspapers in Britain include the Urdu *Daily Jang*, an offshoot of the largest circulation paper in Pakistan, and the Gujarati weeklies, *Garavi Gujarat* and *Gujarat Samachar*. Publications also appear in Bengali (such as the weeklies *Jagoran* and *Janomot*); in Hindi (the weeklies *Amar Deep*, *Hind Samachar* and *Navin Weekly*); and in Punjabi (such as the weeklies *Des Perdes* and *Punjab Darpan* and the monthlies *Rachna* and *Perdesan*).

British provincial newspaper groups are examining the possibilities of printing special editions for their own local ethnic populations. In 1989 the *Leicester Mercury* started publishing a daily Asian edition, incorporating news from the South Asian sub-continent.

The number of black and Asian journalists working on provincial and local London newspapers has increased over recent years, though fewer are found in the national press. In 1989, the editors of national newspapers adopted a code of practice incorporating the requirement that journalists avoid irrelevant references to race, colour and religion—a move welcomed by the Commission for Racial Equality.

The Arts

The last 15 years have seen growing official recognition of the place of ethnic artistic activities in Britain. The Minorities Arts Advisory Service has been established (see p. 86); most regional arts boards have developed contacts with ethnic minority organisations; professional standards have improved; and, instead of reaching only their own particular community, the work of many artists and groups is now seen by wider audiences among the general public.

Financial help for ethnic arts, both traditional and modern, is given mainly by the Arts Council of Great Britain through the regional arts boards, by local authorities and by the Commission for Racial Equality, which has also published related research reports.

Arts Councils

In its report *The Glory of the Garden*, published in 1984, in which the Arts Council of Great Britain set out its strategy for developing the arts for the next ten years, black and Asian dance and drama were identified as areas which would receive additional assistance. The Council has since completed a two-year ethnic minority arts action plan with the publication in 1989 of its report *Towards Cultural Diversity* (see Further Reading, p. 94).

Schemes to encourage cultural diversity have been introduced in a wide range of art forms. In 1989 the Council supported the establishment of a black literary archive, partly based on recorded materials; and in music it was involved in setting up two touring circuits, one promoting the music of Africa and the Caribbean, and the other, that of Asia. Both circuits began touring in mid-1989. In the visual arts, the Council has set up the African and Asian Visual Artists Archive Project. This collates documentation from exhibitions of work by artists of African and Asian origin, provides a resource for students, curators and researchers, and a base for producing new educational materials. The Council has also established Autograph, the Association of Black Photographers, which produces a monthly newsletter and has an exhibition programme and a picture agency featuring the work of black photographers.

The Scottish Arts Council has supported a variety of resident and touring ethnic arts organisations and individual events. It has appointed a Multi-Cultural Arts Officer to work with Scotland's ethnic minorities and to develop a strategy on ethnic arts.

Other Organisations

The Minorities Arts Advisory Service (MAÀS) was set up in 1976 as a national information and resource centre for the arts of the ethnic minority communities. The MAAS helps ethnic arts groups and individuals with advice and information on publicity, fundraising, organising tours, setting up exhibitions and other aspects of arts administration. It also undertakes research and consultancy projects, and community activities. The MAAS Training Unit provides training in arts administration and technical arts skills.

Regular publications include *Artrage*, a quarterly intercultural arts magazine, and *Black Arts in London*, a monthly listings and news journal produced in association with the Arts Media Group. Other MAAS publications include a training bulletin and a touring guide. A national directory of artists and arts groups, with listings of arts resources, funding agencies, venues and educational establishments, has also been compiled.

The Commonwealth Institute also contributes to the encouragement of ethnic arts. It has arranged exhibitions relating to Commonwealth countries and varied programmes of drama, music, dance, film and festival celebrations. The Institute also houses Arts Education for a Multicultural Society. This is a national arts curriculum development project, initiated in 1987, which places artists from culturally diverse backgrounds into schools. Artists work with teachers and pupils in the classroom, and with teachers in staff development and in-service training. Over 550 workshops and residencies by artists took place during 1989–90.

Ethnic Arts Activities

Britain's oldest black theatre company, with one of the busiest touring schedules, is the award-winning Temba. Other prominent companies include Black Theatre Co-operative, Talawa Theatre Company and the Asian group, Tara Arts. In the area of dance, the Black Dance Development Trust and more recently ADiTi, for South Asian dance promotion, are national resource organisations. There has been a growing recognition of the achievements of black and Asian artists and an increase in the number of galleries featuring their work. African,

Caribbean and Asian music now has a broad appeal that is not confined to any particular communities.

Carnival is an activity which forges strong links between the Caribbean and other communities. Inspired by the Trinidad Carnival, the best-known carnival in Britain, at Notting Hill in London, has been described as 'community arts, music, street theatre, community entertainment, multicultural celebration and political statement'.[1] The Notting Hill Carnival, celebrated for the twenty-sixth time in 1991, is recognised as the largest event of its kind in Europe, attracting hundreds of thousands of visitors. The Arts Council makes grants to about 40 carnival clubs and steel bands.

In 1988 a new one-year, postgraduate certificate course on the Asian arts was established, combining the resources of the University of London's School of Oriental and African Studies and Sotheby's Educational Studies. It covers the arts of the Islamic world, China, India, and Japan and the Buddhist world.

---

[1] *The Arts of Ethnic Minorities: Status and Funding.* A research report by the Commission for Racial Equality, 1985.

Addresses

Home Office, 50 Queen Anne's Gate, London SW1H 9AT.

Home Office Immigration and Nationality Department,
Lunar House, Wellesley Road, Croydon CR9 2BY.

Department of Education and Science, Elizabeth House,
York Road, London SE1 7PH.

Department of Employment, Caxton House, Tothill Street,
London SW1H 9NF.

Department of the Environment, 2 Marsham Street, London
SW1P 3EB.

Department of Health, Richmond House, 79 Whitehall,
London SW1A 2NS.

Department of Social Security, Richmond House,
79 Whitehall, London SW1A 2NS.

The Scottish Office, St Andrew's House, Edinburgh
EH1 3BX.

Office of Population Censuses and Surveys, St Catherine's
House, 10 Kingsway, London WC2B 6JP.

Commission for Racial Equality, Elliot House,
10–12 Allington Street, London SW1E 5EH.

Arts Council of Great Britain, 14 Great Peter Street,
London SW1P 3NQ.

British Broadcasting Corporation, Broadcasting House,
London W1A 1AA.

Commonwealth Institute, Kensington High Street, London
W8 6NQ.

Federation of Black Housing Organisations, 374 Gray's Inn Road, London WC1X 8BB.

The Fullemploy Group, County House, 190 Great Dover Street, London SW1 4YB.

Greater London Arts, Coriander Building, 20 Gainsford Street, London SE1 2NE.

Health Education Authority, Hamilton House, Mabledon Place, London WC1H 9TX.

The Housing Corporation, 149 Tottenham Court Road, London W1P 0BN.

Independent Television Commission, 70 Brompton Road, London SW3 1EY.

Metropolitan Police Service, New Scotland Yard, Broadway, London SW1H 0BG.

Minorities Arts Advisory Service, 28 Shacklewell Lane, Fourth Floor, London E8 2EZ.

National Association of Citizens Advice Bureaux, 115 Pentonville Road, London N1 9LZ.

National Council for Voluntary Organisations, 26 Bedford Square, London WC1B 3HU.

National Federation of Housing Associations, 175 Gray's Inn Road, London WC1X 8UP.

National Foundation for Educational Research in England and Wales, The Mere, Upton Park, Slough SL1 2DQ.

National Institute of Adult Continuing Education, 19B De Montfort Street, Leicester LE1 7GE.

Pre-School Playgroups Association, 61–63 King's Cross Road, London WC1X 9LL.

The Runnymede Trust, 11 Princelet Street, London E1 6QH.

Trades Union Congress, Congress House, Great Russell
    Street, London WC1B 3LS.
Windsor Fellowship, 336 Strand, London WC2R 1HB.

Further Reading

Official Publications

Statutes   £

Race Relations Act 1976.
ISBN 0 10 547476 2.   HMSO   1976   6·90

Immigration Act 1971.   Out of
ISBN 0 10 547771 0.   HMSO   1971   print

Immigration Act 1988.
ISBN 0 10 541488 3.   HMSO   1988   2·20

Annual Reports and Statistics

Commission for Racial Equality.   CRE

Control of Immigration:
Statistics, United Kingdom.   HMSO

Immigration and Nationality
Department Report.   Home Office

Other Official Publications

Action not Words. Available from the
National Association of Health Authorities,
Garth House, 47 Edgbaston Park Road,
Birmingham B15 2RS.   1988   12·50

Aspects of Islam in Britain. Foreign &
Commonwealth Office booklet. No 72/90.   FCO   1990   1·50

Bangladeshis in Britain. First Report from the Home Affairs Committee, Session 1986–87.
Vol. 1. ISBN 0 10 271887 3. HMSO 1987 4·70

The Brixton Disorders, 10–12 April 1981. Report of an Inquiry by the Rt Hon the Lord Scarman, OBE. Cmnd 8427.
ISBN 0 10 184270 8. HMSO 1981 9·60

Discrimination in Employment.
First Report from the Employment Committee, Session 1986–87. No 180.
ISBN 0 10 218087 3. HMSO 1987 3·50

Education for All. The Report of the Committee of Inquiry into the Education of Children from Ethnic Minority Groups under the Chairmanship of Lord Swann, FRS, FRSE. Cmnd 9453.
ISBN 0 10 194530 2. HMSO 1985 25·00

'Ethnic origins and the labour market',
in *Employment Gazette*,
Vol 98, March 1990.
ISBN 0 11 728467 X. HMSO 1990 3·80

'The ethnic minority populations of Great Britain: estimates by ethnic group and country of birth', in *Population Trends*,
No 60, Summer 1990.
ISBN 0 11 691279 0. HMSO 1990 6·75

Immigration into Britain. Foreign & Commonwealth Office reference pamphlet.
No 62/90. FCO 1990 2·50

*Race, Community Groups and Service
Delivery.* Home Office Research and
Planning Unit Paper No 113 by Hilary
Jackson and Simon Field.
ISBN 0 11 340972 9.　　　　　　　　　HMSO　1989　　5·30

*Racial Attacks and Harassment. First
Report from the Home Affairs
Committee, Session 1989–90.*
ISBN 0 10 201790 5.　　　　　　　　　HMSO　1989　　7·40

*Racial Attacks and Harassment.
The Government Reply to the First
Report from the Home Affairs Committee,
Session 1989–90.* Cm 1058.
ISBN 0 10 110582 7.　　　　　　　　　HMSO　1990　　2·95

*Racism Awareness Training for the Police:
Report of a Pilot Study by the Home Office.*
Home Office Research and Planning Unit
Paper No 29 by Peter Southgate.　　　　　　　1984　　Free

*The Response to Racial Attacks and Harassment:
Guidance for the Statutory Agencies. Report of
the Inter-Departmental Racial Attacks
Group.*　　　　　　　　　　　　Home Office　1989　　Free

*Tackling Racial Violence and Harassment in
Local Authority Housing: A Guide to Good
Practice for Local Authorities.* Department
of the Environment.
ISBN 0 11 752231 7.　　　　　　　　　HMSO　1989　　4·70

*Towards Cultural Diversity: The Monitoring
Report of the Arts Council's Ethnic Minority
Arts Action Plan.* Arts Council.　　　　　　　1989　　Free

Other Publications

Commission for Racial Equality:

Ageing Minorities: Black People as they Grow Old in Britain.
ISBN 0 907920 81 0.   CRE   1987   Free

The Arts of Ethnic Minorities: Status and Funding. ISBN 0 907920 51 9.   CRE   1985   1·00

Code of Practice for the Elimination of Racial Discrimination in Education.
ISBN 1 85442 023 2.   CRE   1989   1·50

Code of Practice for the Elimination of Racial Discrimination and the Promotion of Equality of Opportunity in Employment.
ISBN 0 907920 29 2.   CRE   1983   2·50

Ethnic Minorities and the Graduate Labour Market.
ISBN 1 85442 024 0.   CRE   1990   2·00

Ethnic Minority School Teachers: a Survey in Eight Local Education Authorities.
ISBN 0 907920 90 X.   CRE   1988   1·00

From Cradle to School: a Practical Guide to Race Equality and Childcare.
ISBN 1 85442 021 6.   CRE   1989   1·00

Juvenile Cautioning and Ethnic Monitoring.
ISBN 1 85442 026 7.   CRE   1990   1·00

Law, Blasphemy and the Multi-Faith Society.
ISBN 1 85442 030 5.   CRE   1990   1·50

*Learning in Terror: a Survey of Racial
Harassment in Schools and Colleges.*
ISBN 0 907920 93 4.   CRE   1988   1·00

*Local Authority Contracts and Racial
Equality: Implications of the Local
Government Act 1988.*
ISBN 1 85442 017 8.   CRE   1989   1·00

A New Partnership for Racial Equality.   Out of
(Policy Document.)   CRE   1989   print

Positive Action and Racial Equality in Housing.
ISBN 1 85442 022 4.   CRE   1989   1·00

*Racial Equality in Social Services
Departments: a Survey of Equal
Opportunities Policies.*
ISBN 1 85442 007 0.   CRE   1990   1·00

*Review of the Race Relations Act 1976:
Proposals for Change.*   Out of
ISBN 0 907920 64 0.   CRE   1985   print

Living Faith in the City.
       General Synod of the Church of England   1990   5·50

WAHAB, IQBAL. *Muslims in Britain:
Profile of a Community.*
ISBN 0 902397 81 8.   Runnymede Trust   1989   1·25

Written by Reference Services,
Central Office of Information.

Printed in the UK for HMSO.
Dd 295008 c40 12/91